TABLE OF CONTENTS

SECTION ONE: Rethinking Retirement

1. Creative Responses to Retirement   10
2. Twelve Retirement Strategies   20
3. Alternative Approaches to Retirment   28
4. Relationships and Retirement   36
5. A Balanced Lifestyle   43
6. Changing Your Lifestyle   48

SECTION TWO: Creative Retirement Projects

7. Projects for the Organizer   66
8. Projects for the Creative Person   96
9. Projects for the Socializer   131
10. Projects for the Intellectual   161
11. Projects for the Volunteer/Caregiver   198
12. Projects for the Nature Lover   222
13. Projects for the Athlete   257
14. Projects for Deferred Retirement   285
15. A Final Thought - Enjoy Yourself   309

Appendix : Travel References For Retirees   315
Index   319

The Complete Guide To a

Creative

Retirement

Robert Kelley

Creative Retirment

ISBN: 0-9740030-9-3

Published by

TurnKey
press

2525 W Anderson Lane, Suite 540
Austin, Texas 78757

Tel: 512.407.8876
Fax: 512.478.2117

E-mail: info@turnkeypress.com
Web: www.turnkeypress.com

ACKNOWLEDGEMENTS

The author is grateful for the assistance provided by the following people who either shared their ideas for suitable hobbies and activities for retirees or evaluated and made suggestions to improve early drafts of the manuscript: Donna Larabie, Joyce Lees, Daniel Goldsmith, Lois and Christ Nichols, Jay and Sandy Harrison, Nancy Scarrow, and Sandra Manuel.

Thanks to Gail Kearns, owner of *To Press and Beyond* in Santa Barbara, California, for manuscript critiquing and editing. Additional copy editing: Nancy Scarrow in Oakville, Ontario, Sandra Manuel, Ohawa, Ontario, and Sara Jenkins of *Present Perfect Books*, Lake Junaluska, North Carolina.

Visual reproductions courtesy of Volk Clip Art, Washington, Illinois. Cover photo courtesy of Comstock Images (www.comstock.com). Chapter quotations by author.

Section One: Rethinking Retirement

1. Creative Responses to Retirement   10
2. Twelve Retirement Strategies   20
3. Alternative Responses to Retirement   28
4. Relationships Altered by Retirement   36
5. Seek a Balanced Lifestyle   43
6. Changing Your Lifestyle   48

Chapter One

Creative Responses to Retirement

Ultimately every retiree is faced with the dilemma of self reinvention.

The December of the first year of my retirement, the local video store phoned and invited me to come into their outlet and pick up a gift certificate, which I did the following evening. When I arrived at the front desk, I told the assistant manager about the phone call and she retrieved an envelope from a drawer and handed it to me.

"What is this for?" I asked.

"It's a gift certificate for $50. You are our highest grossing rental customer," she replied with her best sales clerk smile. "Congratulations, Mr. Kelley."

"Thank you," I replied looking down at the dubious honor. As I left the building, I said to myself, "I got to get a life. I can't spend my evenings just watching videos." I was so embarrassed by the incident that I never did use the gift certificate.

But it did get me thinking about how poorly I was spending my time. I had taken an early retirement from teaching at age fifty and had plenty of opportunities to consider what retirees did with their leisure. I began reading books on the topic, surfing the Internet for helpful websites, and chatting with both happy and unhappy retirees.

What I found were hundreds of books on financial planning, particularly on the art of socking away part of one's earnings for eventual retirement. There are also plenty of research articles on the infirmities of old age and ads for retirement homes for both healthy and disabled seniors. What seemed to be missing were media resources on what relatively young retirees did with their new-found leisure. What did active, healthy, intelligent people do in the two decades following their retirement from a career? The search for answers to that question is what led to the writing of this book.

Countless people dread the very thought of retirement. The idea of retiring from work causes normal, happy commuters and workaholics to stop dead in their tracks with a sudden sense of foreboding, fear, and depression. Rich or poor, high school or college educated, people from all walks of life seem to be equally unprepared for challenges created by the abrupt change of lifestyle.

Retirement can be a bit like being caught in a time warp in which each day appears similar to the day before, something like the characters in the movie *Groundhog Day*. The central character, comedian Bill Murray, is an egocentric weatherman in Punxsutawney, Pennsylvania, covering the Groundhog Day celebrations for a television station. He finds himself in a twenty-four-hour time loop that repeats the same day over and over again for several years. The only redemption for this sad individual involves a complete change in

his cynical, negative outlook on life. He begins to read books, takes piano lessons, gets to know the people in the town, and tries to help as many townspeople as he can during each time loop.

Each retiree is faced with a similar dilemma of self-reinvention. Retirement presents a seemingly endless cycle of twenty-four-hour periods of unplanned holidays, each similar to the one before it. The activities with which people fill those days will ultimately determine the quality of their lives. Those who seek positive, enriching, and helpful activities will find that those activities add up to a happy and worthwhile lifestyle.

For many people in this generation, retirement will be a stretch of time that is equal in length to one's working life, as much as twenty-five to thirty years. People are retiring younger, healthier, wealthier, and better educated. Unlike their parents, they are less inclined to be content with nothing more than to sit at home and dabble in the garden, or babysit the grandkids. This generation is experiencing early retirement because of a number of factors including corporate and government downsizing, company buyouts, corporate mergers, plant closings, company or union pensions that activate at age fifty-five, and investment nest eggs that permit one to choose one's own retirement date. The current average age of retirement in America is fifty-seven. This means that at least half of the population is retiring younger than that. With the post WWII cluster of baby boomers turning fifty at the rate of one every seven seconds, you are going to have lots of company.

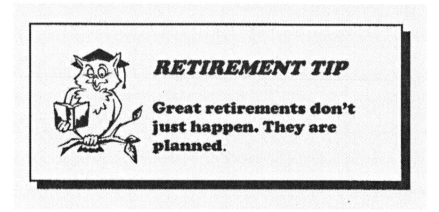

RETIREMENT TIP

Great retirements don't just happen. They are planned.

To the uninitiated, being retired and at leisure seems easy. All you need is the television remote, a comfortable couch, a stack of unread novels, a pile of favorite DVDs, and some snacks. It's our grandparents' equivalent of sitting on the porch in their semi-comfortable cushioned wooden rocking chairs and watching the world go by.

Doing creative things and achieving a sense of fulfillment while retired, however, are much more desirable and attainable goals for today's generation. The differences between most people's actual and potential lifestyles can be quite dramatic. Creative retirement involves passion, emotional commitment, quality of life, and a zest for living. Are you missing any of these things? Is your retirement going the way that you thought it would?

Most people look forward to this part of life with the expectation of having increased leisure time, freedom from time constraints, and freedom to pursue the things that they enjoy. What many people do not expect is the potential emptiness and eventual boredom that often accompanies extensive unplanned leisure time. Spending mornings lounging over coffee in the shopping malls, indulging in impulse buying, taking afternoon naps, watching television, or reading novels about the exciting lives of fictional people certainly passes the time, but it is neither creative nor particularly satisfying. Consider the lifestyle outcomes of the following couple under two different scenarios when one of the spouses is suddenly faced with an unexpected retirement.

Scenario One—An Unplanned Retirement

Ted and Mary Wallace were in their early fifties when the plant where Ted spent the past twenty-eight years working began downsizing and Ted lost his job. He accepted a small early retirement package equal to about half a year's salary. Mary was still working as the office manager of a local insurance company, but feeling burnt out. They owned a two-story, wood-frame, mortgage-free home, and their children were grown up and on their own.

Ted felt lost without a regular daily routine. He began sleeping in later than usual, took afternoon naps while Mary was at work, watched television, cooked the dinners, and did odd jobs around the house. Their social life continued as it had before Ted's layoff. Tuesday evenings Mary went to play bridge with a women's group. Friday evenings were still reserved for bowling with a group of friends, and Sunday afternoon was spent on local excursions to flea markets and dining at out-of-the-way restaurants. After a year, Ted found the boredom of spending days by himself unbearable and began to show signs of depression. He began to look in the newspaper for any job opening that might absorb at least part of his increased leisure time. Instead of adjusting to the new lifestyle, this couple chose to ignore it and continued to respond to the retirement as if nothing had happened.

Scenario Two—A Creative Response

When Ted came home with the news of his unexpected retirement, he and Mary had a long chat about what they might do with the small retirement package, their overall financial circumstances, and how Mary felt about her job. They decided to consider several alternatives over the next few months and bounced ideas off each other. They asked themselves several questions: "What is it that we enjoy doing, but haven't had time for?" "What is it that we are currently doing, but not enjoying?" "Should we continue to live the way we have been, or change our circumstances?" "What can we afford?" As the discussions continued, their enthusiasm over the endless possibilities began to bring smiles to their faces.

A year later, they sold their two-story home and moved into a spacious two-bedroom apartment with a view of a park from their balcony. The combined rent and utility expenses proved to be less than their property taxes, repairs, and heating and electrical bills on their former home. This freed up enough money to purchase a used motor home, and they set off on annual expeditions to combine their interests of traveling, meeting, and chatting with distant relatives. Mary is using her visits with relatives as an opportunity to research and write a book about her family history. They also both took golfing lessons and now enjoy playing at numerous public golf courses during their treks across the country.

Comparing the Scenarios

As you have read in the first scenario, the outcome of not responding to a change in one's lifestyle can lead to depression, restlessness, and unhappiness. If you choose not to be pro-active, retirement can be boring, monotonous, and unimaginative. It is important to recognize that not doing something, that is, not responding to a change in the circumstances in one's life, is "a choice." It is the response of least resistance, the least imagination, and ultimately, the least satisfaction. The alternative, creating a retirement to suit your needs, wants, and desires is hard work. It takes extensive planning and may lead to minor or major changes in one's residence, pursuits, and financial arrangements.

Ted and Mary's second choice may not be the one that you would have picked. But it suited their particular needs and made them happy. There is no fixed or ideal pattern to respond to the circumstances of retirement. Each solution is a personal one and can be endlessly modified to suit your wishes and desires. That's the fun of it. While the first half of your life is devoted to earning a living, daily commuting through dense traffic, paying off the mortgage, and raising and educating your children, the second half of your life can become your reward for services rendered. It's your turn to indulge your wishes and do the things you always wanted to do. It's your turn to enjoy life.

What This Book Will Do for You

This is a book of possibilities. It will help you achieve a fuller, richer, more satisfying life. It will open your eyes to more exciting alternative lifestyles, help you to set goals for yourself, and present a multitude of activities for you to focus on, be involved in, and feel passionate about. It will answer the question most frequently asked by over sixty million retirees in North America: "What will I do with myself today?"

Specifically, Section One of this book will provide you with twelve practical retirement strategies to smooth the transition from the regimented, impersonal world of work to this very personal, open-ended lifestyle of retirement. It will provide five alternative retirement models, including "Leisure and Recreation" and "Altruistic Use of Skills," to see which model suits you the best. It will present four generic case scenarios, which will illustrate that retirement has the potential to alter stable family relationships. It will recommend choosing projects and activities that provide a balanced lifestyle. It will also provide you with retirement work sheets to help you think through and analyze your current needs and wants related to retirement.

The main body of this book, in Section Two, contains eighty delightful projects and activities to enliven and enrich your retirement. To help you select appropriate activities to match your personal set of skills, abilities, and interests, the projects are grouped into eight categories that identify their main focus. The categories include projects for the Organizer, Creative Person, Socializer, Intellectual, Volunteer/Caregiver, Nature Lover, Athlete, and for those who prefer a deferred retirement.

This systematic guide will change your perceptions of traditional retirement. It will broaden your views as to which activities are appropriate for retired people. It will help you to understand why people of the same age may behave in totally different ways even though they have the same resources and similar situations in life. Best of all, it will help you to set personal goals for yourself, to make your retirement an exciting, memorable, and rewarding time in your life. If you are currently a couch potato, maybe it's time to consider making french fries.

RETIREMENT TIP

It is critical to retire to something -- some hobby, activity, past time, or even a part-time job.

Chapter Two

Twelve Retirement Strategies

What people miss most in the early months
of retirement is structure. Their daily routine
has suddenly disappeared and they feel adrift.

Retirement is the only stage of your life that does not prescribe how you are to spend your time. This has not been true during the previous stages of your life. For example, during the twelve to sixteen formative years of your schooling, all of your days were spent in scheduled classes, learning new skills and ideas, being involved in extracurricular activities, and doing homework. During the next thirty to forty years of your adulthood, your days were spent commuting in traffic, working at several jobs, earning a living, and/or raising a family.

In both of these educational and work environments, what you did with your time (with the exception of holidays) was circumscribed and directed by other people. But in the last segment of your life, retirement appears to be a blank screenplay, yet to be written, with you in the role of the writer, the director, and the principal actor. As the writer of the screenplay, you can plan what content is important to you. As the director, you can decide which events are to appear, their sequence, and their frequency. As the main actor, you can decide how much passion, commitment, and energy to devote to various activities.

For the first time in your life, you are going to have to decide what to do with an extra 5,840 hours per year of unscheduled time. This is a lot different than planning what to do on a forty-eight-hour weekend or where to go on an annual two-week vacation. If you have not given much thought to retirement up to this point in your life, this can be a daunting task. It is demoralizing to be faced with nothing to do to fill your time, particularly during long winters or during the gray, dreary rain-filled days of an early spring or late fall.

Given that most of today's retirees are retiring younger and healthier than the previous generation, you are also faced with the possibility of your period of retirement being equal in years to your working years. From that perspective, retirement for many people may stretch twenty or thirty years into the future. That is indeed a large segment of unscheduled and unplanned time.

Consider the following list of twelve practical and complementary short-term retirement strategies. They are designed to help you to smooth the journey from the regimented world of work to a very personal and open-ended retirement lifestyle.

1. Maintain Your Daily Routine

A normal daily routine will help to maintain your sanity and provide a happier outlook on life. Keep your daily routine of eating and sleeping the same. Get up about the same time as you always did and go to bed at the regular time. Nothing can disrupt your sleeping patterns or your digestion more than skipping your traditional breakfast, watching triple late movies, or spending an afternoon napping.

2. Go Out Once a Day

It is important to get out of the household to avoid going stir-crazy. Plan an activity outside your home at least once a day. Make it practical and simple. A trip to the grocery store, pharmacy, clothing store, card shop, hobby shop, building center, car repair center, dentist, doctor, fitness center, weight-loss clinic, or paint and wallpaper store. Many retirees tend to purchase fewer groceries with each trip, but return more frequently. It gets them out of the house and keeps the groceries fresh.

3. Make a Daily Things-To-Do List

To provide some short-term goals, and to make sure that things you want to get done get accomplished, make a things-to-do list each evening before you go to sleep. Make the list short, achievable, and practical.

4. Plan Ahead

At least once a week, consider some of the bigger projects that will take time to implement, or that need appointments, assistance, or special tools to accomplish. These might include getting the rugs steam cleaned, a visit to the dentist, car repairs, hosting a party, repairing the broken fence, planting flowers, purchasing a computer, and getting on the Internet.

Plan the individual steps leading to these events and put them on your things-to-do list.

5. Plan Your Social Life

Social contact is one of the most basic of human needs. When people retire, often their regular daily contact with people suddenly stops. Men in particular need to resocialize as retirees, especially if their after-hour friends have tended to be only colleagues from work. Workplace friendships often diminish over time simply because the social interaction that occurred in the workplace is no longer available.

You may need to reinvent your social life. Ask yourself, "Who can I call?" "Who can I visit?" "What league or organization can I join to meet people?" Seek out relatives, other retirees, volunteer groups, and neighbors. Host a gathering for special occasions such as Halloween or Christmas, card parties, reading clubs, sports nights, block parties, or baby showers for the grandchildren. Plan an interesting trip. Even retirees need a change of pace.

6. Reduce Your Food Intake

In retirement, people are generally less physically active than when they were working full time. Most daily workplace routines involved walking, stair climbing, lifting, carrying, bending, and other activities that burned calories and kept your muscles, heart, and lungs toned. Those routines are gone. Unless you wish to look like a hippopotamus, consider reducing your overall food intake. You might try eating only twice a day instead of three times and eating smaller portions at a sitting. One additional benefit of eating less, according to a study of eighteen hundred Americans by the National Academy of Sciences, is longevity. Even retirees who dieted for the first time in their lives were found to increase their life span and live a healthier life over those who did not.

7. Build Exercise into Your Daily Routine

Muscles and cardiovascular systems tend to atrophy when they are not used. That is why humans tend to get weaker as they get older. Sitting around watching television, or reading a book, or chatting on the telephone are activities that require minimal effort. Find ways to build exercise into your daily activities. Go for a twenty-minute walk. Climb stairs instead of taking the elevator. Park your car at the back of the parking lot and walk to the mall. Join a health fitness club and exercise all the muscles in your body three times a week. Take a swim fitness class and do your exercises in the water. Go for a hike in the woods and let the fresh air into your lungs. If you do any of these activities, most likely your energy and endurance will increase, and you will sleep more soundly.

8. Simplify Your Life

You have accumulated a lifetime of objects, trinkets, outdated appliances, and perhaps clothing that no longer fits. Maybe it's time to consider having a garage sale, making donations to a goodwill association, or throwing stuff out. Get rid of the clutter in your life. Simplify. Keep the things that are useful and remove the rest.

9. Indulge Your Favorite Hobbies

Most people have favorite pastimes that they enjoy doing when time permits. When you worked full time
these were the activities that you used to look forward
to on weekends or on annual vacations: visiting people,
camping, golfing, working on your family history,
coaching a little league team, oil painting, playing the
piano, or gardening. Make them the centerpieces in
your retirement. Spend time doing the things that you
enjoy.

10. Improve Your Retirement Skills

Just because you were skillful and successful during
your full-time career does not mean that you will automatically become talented in your chosen pursuits,
hobbies, and pastimes in retirement. What made you
good at your previous employment was repetitive training, theory courses, skill-building workshops, weekend retreats, and on-the-job practice. Retirement is
no different. If you expect to suddenly become a golf
pro, a published writer, or an expert painter simply
because you are retired with time to spare, you may
be in for a rude awakening. New hobbies take time to
learn.

Fortunately, there are workshops and courses on prac-
tically every hobby that you can imagine, each designed
to help you hone your skills. Do your research. Write
for workshop brochures or lists of evening school hobby
courses or college catalogs. Scan the advertisements
in your favorite hobby magazines and find out where
adult workshops or conferences are being conducted.
Talk to other hobbyists. Search the Internet for schools

and colleges in North America that are willing to provide you with the expertise you need. Do not be afraid to travel to attend a multiple-day workshop. Local institutions cannot be expected to provide everything.

11. Find a Support Group

You are not the first person to be retired. Nor are you the only person to work on a particular hobby or project. Virtually every activity of human endeavor has a support group with people of similar interests who will share your enthusiasm for your favorite pastime. There are associations with monthly newsletters and meetings for people who enjoy sailing, traveling in motorhomes, and motorcycling; for poets, writers, artists, photographers, and musicians; for family history researchers, bird watchers, gardeners; people who love cooking; as well as book-critique groups, chess clubs, volunteer agencies, and religious groups. The list is endless.

Begin your research. Find out where a support group is available for your hobby. Talk to people who enjoy the activity and ask them where they go for help. Study the ads in hobby magazines. Search the Internet for established national or regional associations or converse with hobby enthusiasts in an Internet chat room.

12. Lose Yourself in Your Projects

When the late comedian George Burns reached his hundredth birthday, people asked him what he thought contributed to his longevity. "Probably having something to look forward to each day has helped," he replied. "It gives you a reason for getting out of bed every morning." Most daily activities, such as shopping, watching television, washing the dishes, or reading the newspaper help to pass the time. But what retirees need in their lives are large projects that challenge them emotionally, physically, and intellectually. What things in life are you passionate about? Volunteering? Organizing some event? Being creative? Using your hands? Traveling? Being around people? Seek out activities that get you involved, excited, and happy. Keep in mind that extraordinary lives are lived by ordinary people who have an extraordinary passion for something greater than themselves.

Chapter Three

Alternative Approaches to Retirement

*Retirement is an opportunity to set new goals
and to head in new directions.*

Not everyone envisions the last segment of their life in the same way. Some people take a traditional approach, following the example set by their parents. Some see retirement as an opportunity to set new goals and head in new directions. That's why the activities of retirees can vary immensely. One person might enjoy outdoor hiking and traveling. Another person might be engrossed in researching and writing a book, while a third individual might enjoy volunteering at an archeological site helping to uncover dinosaur bones.

It may be helpful for you to consider five alternative approaches to retirement before you make a decision on what to do with your time. Each approach can be enjoyable and satisfying. There is no right or wrong choice. What differentiates the following models is their increasing levels of creativity, complexity, sense of purpose, and personal fulfillment for the individuals involved.

1. Deferred Retirement

Some people cannot picture themselves as being at leisure and choose not to retire. They instead defer retirement until ill health or catastrophe strikes and forces them to quit work. This "Work Till I Drop" mode, reminiscent of the cowboy who wants to "die with his boots on," is not readily available to everyone. Self-employed individuals, such as doctors with private practices, politicians, lawyers, dentists, accountants, consultants, writers, artisans, and entrepreneurs, face far less resistance to continued work than corporate or civil service, military, or plant shop employees.

Money is usually the major factor for deferred retirement. An impoverished individual who is working to bridge the income gap between forced retirement and the onset of a retirement pension may immediately seek another job. Parents near retirement with children still in college may choose to continue working to assist their offspring with tuition. These people may wish to retire early, but just cannot afford it.

Another common motivation for retirees continuing to work is boredom. Having a job is a guaranteed way to get them out of the house and doing something useful. Work provides immediate structure to one's day, goal-oriented tasks to perform, and socialization with other people—all the things retirees seek.

Several additional things may motivate people to defer their retirement, including job satisfaction, a desire to achieve something special, a desire to complete a particular task or goal, or an unwarranted fear of retirement based perhaps on a perception that their self-worth is directly dependent on being a productive, purposeful member of society. Any of these factors may cause a recent retiree to immediately seek a new job, even if it's simply working as a security guard or as an fast-food employee earning subsistence wages.

2. Leisure and Recreation

The most frequent perception that working people have of retirement is that it's a stretch of time that is to be devoted entirely to leisure, the pursuit of hobbies, and moderate recreational activities. The main idea is avoid any activity that resembles traditional work. This image of the contented leisure-class retiree is reinforced by today's retirement magazines that project a lifestyle of recreation, relaxation, and leisure activities, while their advertisements attempt to sell you vitamins, pain relievers, running shoes, large comfortable luxury cars, and residence in some community-living retirement village. A similar image is projected by television advertisements offering mutual fund investments, insurance protection, and "freedom 55" early-retirement concepts.

The type of activities pursued often depends on the retiree's level of disposable income. For example, people with high incomes may seek leisurely retreats at exclusive resorts or health spas, play tennis and golf, do some horseback riding, yachting, and sunbathing on a beach in the Caribbean. Winter ski lodges, world cruises, and extended vacations to exotic locations are also popular pastimes.

People with more moderate incomes may be involved in activities such as golfing, painting, gardening, walking, birdwatching, reading, and occasionally taking extended vacations to warmer climates, or visiting distant children and grandchildren. Traveling is one of the most popular pastimes of retirees.

Generally, recreational sporting activities pursued by retirees are low-impact and noncompetitive and may include fishing, biking, nature hiking, swimming, water aerobics, dancing, waterskiing, cross-country skiing, and ski-dooing. Competitive activities are often restricted to leisurely games of golf and tennis. Occasionally, some retirees may seek to include brief flirtations with slightly higher-risk behavior, such as a parachute jump out of an airplane, a ride in a hot-air balloon, white-water rafting, or rock climbing.

3. Unfinished Business

Other people choose their activities based on an altogether different motivation. These are the people who know that this is their one last chance to do something they always wanted to do, but were too busy, too poor, or too frightened to try it during the earlier portion of their lives. It's the unfinished business of their past being played out during their retirement years.

For example, Fran Keeler, who was a successful salesperson as a teenager, gets married, pregnant and quits work to become a housewife. Fran secretly felt cheated of the opportunity to see what she could have accomplished in the business world. Now that the children and husband are gone, she plans and starts her own business retail store and throws all her passion and commitment behind the project to make it a success.

Edward Fisher, a retired advertising copywriter for a major marketing firm, has always held the dream of writing the great American novel. That was why he chose an undergraduate university degree in English literature. Between the pressures of his job and raising a family in the suburbs, there never seemed to be any time to write. At age fifty-eight, Ed purchased a new computer and laser printer and now his wife complains to neighbors that he continues to work on the project into the wee hours of the morning.

Jayne Fillman, a single retired woman, lives alone. For forty years she worked in a low-paying office job and lived in an urban tenement building and wished that she could go on fabulous holidays like other people talked about, but that she could never afford. After some research, she discovered that airlines offer low air fares for seniors, and her local ladies' church group had organized a "last-minute travel club" to take advantage of empty seats on holiday package flights. "Now let's see, where did I put my bathing suit?" Jayne said to herself, as she packed her bag for her fourth trip.

4. Leaving a Legacy

Robert Ferguson, a man in his mid-fifties, once confessed to friends at his cottage that he felt he never amounted to much and that he never accomplished anything of importance in his life. This overwhelming feeling remained with him in spite of his friends who consoled him and reminded him of his two healthy children, both university graduates, who were doing well financially; his comfortable cottage that he built himself from scratch; and his numerous acquisitions, including a new car. For some people, leaving a legacy becomes a strong motivating factor in their choice of retirement activities. They feel a deep-rooted desire to leave something of lasting importance for the world to remember them by after they are gone.

One of the greatest realizations that keeps creative minds alive and flourishing at an advanced age, and often until the moment of death, is the knowledge that their work will outlive them. The legacies themselves can take many different forms. For example, a retiree lovingly pens his memoirs to leave to his grandchildren. A seventy-five-year-old artist takes six months to paint a huge colorful landscape mural on the wall of a municipal office building. A grandmother learns to use a computer to write uplifting children's stories for electronic publication on the Internet. An old man spends weeks carving intricate wooden figurines to give as gifts to his friends and relatives. All of these people hope to be remembered fondly when people view the creative accomplishments that they left behind.

5. Altruistic Use of Skills

A fifth retirement model involves the continued use of one's work-related skills, but with a different goal. Instead of money, power, achievement, or wealth being the primary motivating factor in one's activities, one substitutes altruism, compassion, or a desire to give something back to society. The more that an individual's motives focus attention on other people's needs, or on lasting helpful achievements, or on financial or political causes that benefit humanity in some way, the greater the satisfaction, sense of purpose, and fulfillment in life will be.

Here are eight examples of how a person's previous work skills can continue to be used in an altruistic way in retirement. The politician becomes a mentor for a political hopeful. The financier becomes a hospital fund raiser. The athlete becomes the community's little league coach. The office manager organizes volunteers at a local food bank. The construction worker refurbishes old apartments for the homeless. The successful entrepreneur advises people starting their first business. The former teacher organizes a campaign to prevent erosions in educational funding. The veterinarian becomes an animal rights activist.

Conclusion: Personalize Your Own Retirement

As the five alternative approaches to retirement presented in this chapter indicate, there are a variety of ways to live the last segment of your life. You may recognize your own pattern emerging within them. It may explain why one retired neighbor is gardening, while another neighbor of the same age is passionately involved in operating a business. There are no right or wrong choices, but the choice is a very personal one. To find happiness, you must consider matching your activities to your own wishes, needs, and desires.

Copying the hobbies or activities of your spouse, neighbor, or best friend may help to pass the time, but probably won't leave you with any personal feelings of satisfaction or fulfillment. There are no "other chances" after this part of your life. In your next reincarnation, you may return as a cute little chipmunk or a mean-spirited badger and never have the opportunity to discover if you liked playing golf, or liked photographing kangaroos in Australia, or enjoyed helping an archeological team dig up dinosaur bones.

Chapter Four

Relationships and Retirement

Retirement requires social readjustments,
not just with external friendships but
also between marital partners.

Recent television commercials aimed at retirees presented the image of a white-haired couple holding hands and walking barefoot on an exotic sandy beach, their healthy, trim bodies silhouetted in black against a beautiful setting sun. The reality for many couples, however, can be quite different, and in many cases, retirement may bring feelings of frustration, anger, depression, and isolation. Nationally, the rate of divorce shows a sharp spike at two times during the course of a lifetime. One is in the first five years of marriage. The other, surprisingly, is just after retirement. Here's how it can happen.

For the first time in thirty or forty years of married life, some couples find themselves home with each other twenty-four hours a day. There are no children to distract the "empty-nesters," no jobs to take them away for part of the day, and they have nothing particularly planned for retirement other than rest and relaxation. No matter how much these people like each other, this situation can be a recipe for disaster.

Retirement is a different segment of life that requires reinvention of one's goals, expectations, and pursuits. It also requires social readjustments, not just with new external friendship patterns to replace those lost at work, but more importantly, readjustments in behavior and expectations between spouses and partners. Retirement not only alters your daily routine, but also changes the subtle interpersonal relationships between those living in the household. To illustrate how retirement can affect the dynamics of previously stable relationships, consider the following four cases.

Case One—The Unwanted Shadow

Margaret and Fred Langdon live in a four-bedroom home nestled on a street lined with oak and maple trees in a mature urban suburb. Margaret has spent her life as a homemaker, raising the children through their early years, proud of her neat house, attractive flower garden, and her ability to cook great-tasting meals from scratch. She is a volunteer at the local hospital and a member of the neighborhood women's bridge club that meets one afternoon a week. Fred worked as the assistant manager of the accounting department at a major department store and recently retired on a company pension. Fred, who is a quiet, private individual, doesn't have any hobbies and had spent most of his thirty-year career working six days a week. Suddenly he is home full time with no hobby interests and few domestic or repair skills. So he offers Margaret his help around the kitchen, making little suggestions, such as what spices to add to her soups and meats and that maybe the dried glassware would be better stored upside down on the shelves to prevent dust from getting in, and what flowers might look nice in her prized flower garden. His social life had been re-stricted to colleagues from work, and they are no longer around to invite him for lunch or a beer after closing time. Now he watches sports on television and does a little reading. He drives Margaret to the grocery store and to her card game because he has nothing better to do. He is happy just to be in the company of his wife.

Margaret's emotional state is quite different. Where she once had independence, freedom of movement, and complete control of her household, she now has a twenty-four-hour shadow that follows her everywhere like a lost puppy. His kitchen suggestions ring in her ear as criticisms, and his constant companionship becomes a ball and chain and too much for her to bear. Within two years, Margaret files for a divorce and leaves poor stay-at-home Fred in a state of shock and disbelief.

Case Two—Different Expectations

Maria and Carmen Mattina both worked outside the home for the greater part of their marriage. Maria worked as a floral arranger and salesperson in a flower shop while Carmen operated his own hairstyling business. Both worked long hours, six days a week. Their four children are now adults and out on their own. Maria and Carmen are accustomed to seeing each other mainly for late dinners and on weekends. When Carmen reached sixty-five, he sold the business and retired on the proceeds of the sale along with a monthly government pension. Maria, at age sixty, quit her job, and for the first time in their marriage they find themselves alone with each other twenty-four hours a day.

Carmen seeks distraction by playing golf several days a week, meeting in the shopping mall food court in the afternoons to sip coffee and chat with old friends, and watching baseball, hockey, and basketball on television in the evenings. Maria grows depressed and non-talkative even during the brief occasions when they get together.

Sensing something is amiss, Carmen asks Maria "What's wrong?" Maria breaks out in tears and explains that she has been willing to put up with not being together while raising the kids and working full time, but now that they are retired, she wants to rekindle the romance that she felt when they were first married. She wants to hold hands, take walks on the beach, and experience the warmth and love she felt was lost while they were both earning enough money to raise their large family. Carmen thinks of retirement as an extension of the independent existence he had lead throughout his working career. They have different expectations, which need to be expressed and clarified and negotiated, if they intend to stay together.

Case Three—Forced into Retirement

Wally Beecham, at age fifty-two, had worked at the local auto assembly for twenty-seven years when he hears the news. The head office is downsizing production of one of their least successful models, and Wally's plant is reduced from three shifts to one. The non-unionized workforce have no seniority clause, and all employees over the age of fifty are the first to be let go. Wally is emotionally devastated. He always considered himself to be the primary breadwinner, even though his wife Brenda works full time as an assistant office manager. In addition to a loss of income, Wally also feels a loss of social status and self-respect. This is on top off the changes that an ordinary retirement brings into a family, including the loss of a daily routine, loss of physical exercise from the workplace, and loss of the social network of friends that the auto plant provided during and after work.

Wally's frustration over his layoff turns into anger, which he vents upon Brenda in the form of criticisms, sarcasm, and insults in the months that follow. Before Wally can deal with the substantial lifestyle changes that retirement brings into a household, he has to learn first to deal with the altered self-image and raw emotions triggered by the layoff. Brenda tires of waiting for the healing process to begin and files for a divorce. She has no desire to spend retirement with this angry person.

Case Four—Retiring Single From a Career

Lisa Hartman earned a college business degree as a young woman and enjoyed working in the human resources departments of several large corporations before retiring as a department director on a company buyout and pension. Lisa did not look forward to retirement. Because of her frequent career moves to different cities, she never developed a circle of lasting friendships. She also never had time to develop any hobbies or activities outside her career. Now, at age sixty, Lisa feels bored, isolated, depressed, and a little frightened of the endless series of unstructured days that lay ahead. She turns to drinking wine to dull the reality.

Individuals who concentrate on their career as the main focus in their life often neglect to develop the interests, friendships, and hobbies that help to make retirement an enjoyable journey. They can feel an enormous sense of discontinuity and purposelessness when their career comes to an end. For them, retirement requires a complete reinvention of their lifestyle and will involve exploration, risk-taking, rebuilding of routines, and a sense of adventure.

Responding to Altered Conditions

As the above four cases indicate, retirement can dramatically alter stable family relationships. This often comes as a surprise to the participants who don't realize that the conditions and reasons for the relationship have permanently changed. The partners' expectations of each other under these new conditions need to be discussed and the relationship itself may need to be renegotiated.

The worst-case scenario is often a forced retirement in which one of the partners is laid off work. So in addition to the typical loss of daily structure, social contacts, healthy physical and mental activities, the individual often suffers from anger and frustration. Couples in this situation should consider seeking help from a family therapist to resolve the anger issues before making any plans for a new lifestyle.

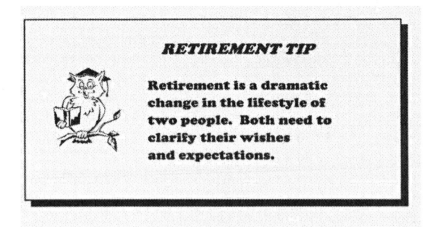

RETIREMENT TIP

Retirement is a dramatic
change in the lifestyle of
two people. Both need to
clarify their wishes
and expectations.

Chapter Five

A Balanced Lifestyle

*Retirees can achieve greater happiness and
contentment by simply including four basic
elements in their lifestyle.*

After an early period of experimentation, which may
average from two to four years, most people eventually
settle for a small cluster of retirement activities with
which they feel comfortable. The activities will generally suit their level of income, be easily accessible, and
require a minimal of physical and intellectual effort. A
couple may take up gardening, dabble in oil painting,
read novels, take a car trip to visit relatives during the
summer, or babysit the grandchildren. These particular activities are home-centered, inexpensive, and low
stimulus. They are choices resulting from the application of minimal effort and from ignoring creative thinking. Ultimately, the choices may lead to restlessness,
depression, and unhappiness. However, retirement
doesn't have to be an endless series of similar days.
Creating an alternative retirement to suit your needs,
wants, and desires is hard work, but is a much more
worthwhile goal.

It may be helpful to have some general guidelines to
assist you with the selection of projects that will
provide a balanced lifestyle.

Creative Retirement

Nourishing the Mind

The mind requires active intellectual stimulation to keep from getting bored and depressed. Watching hours of television, quiet knitting, or reading romance/adventure novels certainly passes the time, but does little to stimulate brain activity. Those are relatively passive activities, intellectually rated just slightly above sitting in a rocking chair. What about your organizational, creative, intuitive, leadership, and problem-solving skills? How are you exercising them? Brain cells wither from lack of use. You progressively suffer from forgetfulness, slowness of speech, and increasingly muddled thinking. One inevitable fact of life is, what does not get used, nature takes away.

Nourishing the Body

The body requires active physical stimulation to keep bones and muscles from atrophying. Like an astronaut returning from a long gravity-free space jaunt, you will discover that your body grows progressively weaker when physical activities diminish. The human body is designed to adapt to whatever environment and lifestyle you present to it. If you choose to be a couch potato, watching endless hours of television, drinking beer, and eating snack foods, expect your body to grow fatter and weaker. If you choose to spend part of each day walking, swimming, or bicycling, expect your body to grow leaner and stronger.

BALANCED LIFESTYLE

What is a balanced lifestyle? Simple. You need to pursue a cluster of activities that satisfy four basic elements: the mind, the body, the soul, and the human need for social interaction with the world around you.

Nourishing the Soul

Everyone needs to feed their soul, that part of themselves which defines who they are as a person. It needs nourishment much like your physical body needs food for fuel. But what does a soul need to nourish it? The answer is, it depends on the individual's character. Compassionate people nourish their souls by helping an elderly neighbor with her chores and volunteering for charity fund raising. Achievement-driven people nourish their souls by the completion of a complex set of tasks. Helpful, sharing people nourish their souls by teaching others new skills.

"Soul food" may also come from gardening, the feeling of being one with the earth and the miracle of creating life from nothing more than soil, water, and seed. It may come from caring for abused and abandoned cats and dogs at the local animal center. It may come from work with a religious institution and a feeling of closeness to God. Nourishing the soul is a very personal act

45

that touches you deeply, emotionally, and gives you inner peace.

Nourishing the Need for People

The last of the four elements of a balanced lifestyle relates to the human need for social interaction with the world around you. It involves reaching out beyond your own household to people, organizations, and institutions in a social context. The daily interaction with a variety people and the social functions that used to be provided by your former workplace have disappeared. You need to find new people with whom to share your activities and projects. The old adage "No man/woman is an island" reminds you that social contact is the most basic of human needs. Friends praise your accomplishments, listen to your troubles, and lend a helping hand when necessary.

People also affirm your existence. You may create the most useful and beautiful artifact in the world. But if no one is around to admire it, becomes a shallow achievement. Like a tree falling in the forest with no one there to see it, the event goes unnoticed. Change that situation. Get noticed. Two people make a better card game than one. Four people can make it a social event complete with sandwiches, chips, beverages, and the promise of interaction beyond the card game. Talk to people. Join a hobby group. Write for an Elderhostel traveling/learning catalog. Share your love of a favorite project, such as cooking, outdoor camping, antique furniture restoration, researching family history, or traveling to exotic places that start with the letter "A."

Your retirement years may be a period of time that lasts as long as your working years. How you spend your days will determine your quality of life. With a little planning, some creative thinking, and some risk-taking, it just may contain some of the happiest and most rewarding moments you have yet to experience. Think of it as an intriguing journey, full of promise and opportunity. Climb into the saddle of your favorite steed (Mustang, Bronco, or other wild animal), adjust your hat, take the reins in your capable hands, and ride off into the morning sunrise in search of new and exciting adventures. There are lots of them out there.

Chapter Six

Changing Your Lifestyle

*A person without goals is a person
who is unlikely to reach any.*

Planning is the key to unlocking a new and rewarding lifestyle. In retirement, you are faced with an endless series of choices. One choice is to become a household vegetable—an unmovable couch potato or a limp tabletop turnip basking in the sun. It's quite easy to visualize. Just don't make any plans for tomorrow or the next day. Get up late. Watch some soap operas or talk shows on television. Putter around the house. Get depressed watching the news. Time will surely pass. Days will grow into weeks, weeks into months, months into years. Finally, on your death bed, you will whisper to a disinterested nurse who is busy tending her chores, "I think that I just wasted the best years of my life. My choices were unlimited, but I chose to do none of them." If that's not what you want engraved on your epitaph, perhaps you might want to consider more exciting alternatives.

Creative retirement requires some reflective thinking on the type of activities you consider to be the most important in your life. What brings you the most happiness: family ties, friendships, social relationships, helping others, keeping healthy and fit, being constantly active, quiet leisure time, being creative, making things with your hands, reading about new things, visiting new places? They all sound great, but most people will consistently place higher value on just a few of these items throughout their lifetime. This chapter is designed to clarify, identify, and prioritize which activities you value the most and help you to set personal goals to strive toward in retirement. Those activities that you value and deem important should be the cornerstones and foundations of your retirement because they will automatically bring you the most happiness, fulfillment, and satisfaction.

This chapter will help you begin to analyze what it is that you want out of life. It will also help you to identify which things are important to you and which are not.

The following section contains a work sheet with sixteen questions. Get a pen or pencil, and be prepared to think through and respond to the questions. No one is peeking, so you can be as honest and open as you wish. Your answers may surprise you. Don't be afraid to leave a question and come back to it later. There is no time limit and there are no right or wrong answers. This is a personal analysis of your current situation in anticipation of retirement.

Creative Retirement

A Work Sheet for Analyzing Your Needs

Part One—Identifying Activities You Enjoy

1. List five activities that you enjoy doing, or that
   you would like to be doing, even if you have not
   had the time to pursue them until now. Then
   write what is it that you like about each activity
   listed.

a)_____

_____

_____

_____

b)_____

_____

_____

_____

c)_____

_____

_____

_____

d)_____

_____

_____

_____

e)_____

_____

_____

_____

2. From the list below, circle the words that best describe the types of activities that you enjoy the most.

Organizing   Socializing

Creative   Nature Lover

Intellectual   Athletic

Continue   Volunteer/
Working   Caregiver

3. Suggest one activity, hobby, or pastime that you might enjoy doing for each of the activity categories circled in the previous question.

a)_____

b)_____

c)_____

d)_____

4. From the list of fifteen items provided below, indicate with a check mark five activities that would best reflect what you value the most at this point in your life. Then, rank each of the five items in importance by numbering them from 1 (most important) to 5 (least important).

FAMILY RELATIONSHIPS _____
(sons, daughters, siblings grandchildren, nieces, nephews)

 SOCIAL RELATIONSHIPS _____
(neighbors, bowling team, book club, bridge club)

INSTITUTIONAL RELATIONSHIPS _____
(hospital, school, fraternities, religious/cultural group)

LEAVING A LEGACY *(for other people)* _____
(crafts, carvings. paintings, buildings, family history books)

WORKING WITH YOUR HANDS _____
(cooking, gardening, repairs, building furniture, restoring antiques, making pottery)

LEARNING NEW THINGS _____
(courses, workshops, self-help books, hobbies, musical instruments)

ORGANIZING EVENTS _____
(parties, anniversaries, birthdays, reunions, political activities, trips)

QUIET LEISURE TIME _____
(knitting, reading, watching TV, surfing the Internet)

TRAVELING _____
(car trips, motorhomes, cruises, learning vacations)

HELPING OTHERS _____
(volunteering, canvassing, visiting shut-ins, charity work, physical labor)

EARNING MONEY _____
(part-time job, home-based business, full-time job)

ENJOYING THE OUTDOORS _____
(gardening, camping, fishing, nature walks, birding, nature photography)

BEING CREATIVE _____
(painting, crafts, writing, music, cooking, decorating)

KEEPING PHYSICALLY FIT _____
(walking, aerobics, weight-training, bike riding, jogging, swimming, dancing, skiing)

5. For each of the numbered items checked and ranked above, give one or more examples of hobbies or activities related to them that you would enjoy doing.

a) _____

b) _____

c) _____

d) _____

e) _____

Summary—Activities You Enjoy

Several things should be coming clear from the first five questions. There are certain activities that you, as an individual, place value on in your life. You have categorized and ranked them in importance. You have also identified specific activities that you enjoy doing the most and categorized them. This is important to the use of this book. The clearer the understanding you have of the categories of activities that are preferable to you, the easier it is to select other projects that have those same characteristics, and which should also give you happiness and satisfaction in their performance.

Part Two—Identifying Accommodation Needs

1. Do you enjoy living where you are at present?

   _____

2. Why or why not? _____

   _____

   _____

   _____

   _____

3. Check off your preference of places to live during retirement.

   _____ Remain in present home

   _____ Sell home and move elsewhere

   _____ Keep both a summer and winter residence

4. If you desired ownership of a second place of residence for vacations or seasonal getaways, which would you prefer, given your financial circumstances (check one or more choices).

_____ Cottage

_____ Permanent Trailer Park

_____ Mobile Home or Motorhome

_____ Condominium

_____ Time-Share Resort

_____ Other (specify) _____

5. Identify your vacation preferences now that you are retired.

_____ Stay around home

_____ Vacation in same location each year

_____ Vacation varies with each trip

_____ Interchangeable resort package

6. Considering your expected retirement lifestyle, describe an ideal place to live during retirement.

_____

_____

_____

7. Suggest changes in accommodations that may be needed to achieve an ideal place to live during retirement.

_____

_____

_____

_____

Summary—Accommodation Needs

Retirement brings a number of changes in your lifestyle. Children are grown and have left several rooms empty in the family household. Your income has diminished, and the maintenance and costs of operating a full-size home are becoming too expensive relative to income. Your health may be slowly deteriorating and the physical requirements of cleaning, repairing, cutting the lawn, and clearing the leaves or snow is becoming too onerous. You may have become tired of living all year in the snow belt, or in a neighborhood that has declined in safety and economic status.

WHAT ONE COUPLE DID

A creative Arizona couple with grown children sold their home in Phoenix and moved into their cottage in Flagstaff when they retired. The also bought a sixty-foot motorhome and for several months each year, they drove all across America sight-seeing and visiting relatives.

It may be time to consider changing your residence. Is it time to downsize? Is a southern getaway an attractive proposition? Is a year-round cottage, a mobile home, or a move out of your neighborhood to a more retirement-friendly environment worth considering? Should you consider moving closer to siblings, children, or grandchildren? These are questions that you should be asking yourself.

One interesting statistical fact is that there are increasing numbers of retirees moving from big cities to small towns. Homes are cheaper in smaller towns. Communities are more peaceful. There is less crime, less immigration, less change in small towns. They tend to be more homogeneous with greater number of retirees with similar values.

Another possibility worth considering are the new self-contained retirement villages being built across America. These enclosed communities often have choices in type of residence, active community centers with dances, fitness classes, instruction in crafts, banquet facilities, as well as walking trails, day excursions by bus and the company of people your own age.

Creative Retirement

Part Three—Living Comfortably in Retirement

1. What items in your life need to be acquired
   to enhance the quality of your lifestyle? Check
   one or more items.

_____ Purchase, repair, or upgrade your car

_____ Purchase or upgrade a computer

_____ Become computer literate

_____ Purchase leisure clothing

_____ Kitchen remodeling

_____ Landscaping

_____ Patio deck

_____ Swimming pool

_____ Develop a hobby room

_____ Refurbish living room

_____ Air conditioning

_____ Heating system

2. What improvements could be made to your health and physical fitness to make retirement more enjoyable?

_____ Dental work

_____ Foot exam

_____ Eye exam

_____ Hearing exam

_____ Weight reduction

_____ Increase in physical fitness

3. What specific areas need to be improved to become more physically fit? Check one or more items.

_____ Flexibility

_____ Strength

_____ Stamina

_____ Weight loss

4. List three specific lifestyle changes that may be possible for you to achieve this year.

a) _____

b) _____

c) _____

d) _____

Summary—Living Comfortably

The previous four questions should help you to identify items in your life that need changing, to ensure that your retirement will be comfortable, enjoyable, and bring you some measure of happiness. Changes might include improvements to your household to increase efficiency and comfort, throwing out stuff that is no longer useful, lifestyle adjustments to enhance your health and well being, and setting short-term goals.

Your needs will change over time. You will achieve some of your goals and discard others in favor of new ones, depending on your personal circumstances. Revisit this questionnaire six months from now and re-evaluate your answers

Section Two: Creative Retirement Projects

7. Projects for the Organizer   56
8. Projects for the Creative Person   103
9. Projects for the Socializer   121
10. Projects for the Intellectual   151
11. Projects for the Volunteer/Caregiver   188
12. Projects for the Nature Lover   212
13. Projects for the Athlete   247
14. Projects for Deferred Retirement   275
15. A Final Thought—Enjoy Yourself   292

Introduction to This Section

The next eight chapters offer eighty exciting projects for you to consider pursuing in retirement. The projects are organized into eight categories that describe their essential characteristics: Organizer, Creative Person, Socializer, Intellectual, Volunteer/Caregiver, Nature Lover, Athlete, and the Deferred Retirement type.

The opening to each chapter has a short definition of the kind of person who would enjoy the activities presented within the chapter. Beneath the definition is a list of ten projects with a check box beside each one, which allows you to check off only the projects that are of personal interest. This is followed by detailed descriptions of each project with suggestions on how to implement them, as well as resources that include books, videotapes, DVDs, audio cassettes , and Internet web sites.

The following chapters are not meant to be read sequentially. After completing your work sheet analysis in Chapter Six, you should have circled two or three categories that identify the types of projects in which you are already interested. Choose one of the circled categories, then turn directly to the chapter with that particular title. Read through the list of suggested topics to see if you can find one that seems interesting and read up on it. Choose another circled category from the work sheet and turn to the projects within the chapter with that particular title.

Keep in mind that most people tend to follow the same sort of interests as they did on weekends or while on vacation when they were working full time. Concentrate all your efforts on just two or three major activities. Choose ones that seem exciting and appear worth a commitment of your time and effort. Choose combinations of projects that provide a balance in life. Those are the projects that will bring a sense of purpose, satisfaction, and fulfillment in your retirement.

Chapter Seven

Projects for the Organizer

Organizers get the most enjoyment out of life when they are arranging, scheduling, and preparing for some special event. They are active, task-oriented individuals whose favorite phrase is, "I love it when things come together!" Their goals may be as simple as arranging for a young niece's birthday party or as complex as organizing a national conference for retirees. The challenge of bringing some event to fruition is their source of happiness. This chapter presents ten projects for the retired person who loves to organize. Check off the projects that you might be interested in.

Projects in This Chapter: ✔

1. Organize a Family Reunion ☐
2. Start a Social Activity Committee ☐
3. Teach a Hobby Course ☐
4. Plan a Group Trip ☐
5. Have a Garage Sale ☐
6. Remodel Your Retirement Home ☐
7. Plan an Extended Vacation ☐
8. Organize a Supper Club ☐
9. Visit the Wonders of the World ☐
10. House Swap ☐

Project One—Organize A Family Reunion

If you enjoy the company of your relatives and like being with family members, you might consider organizing a family reunion. The scale of the event will depend on how many relatives you intend to invite. It may include only descendants of one brother and his wife; it may extend to an entire branch of the family tree going back to your grandparents; it may encompass the entire family tree going back several generations and involve hundreds of relatives from several different branches.

A small informal reunion of twenty to thirty people might be held at someone's house or cottage during the summer. The day might be used to celebrate a significant wedding anniversary, with a backyard barbecue or a potluck supper, and an opportunity for people to chat with each other while sitting in their lawn chairs or gathered around the buffet table. The small reunion can be organized easily by one or two people with invitations made by telephone or by mail at least two months in advance.

A larger more formal reunion could take place at a rented hall with a catered dinner and include head table speeches, a dinner, and a dance, similar to a wedding reception. People might dress for the occasion.

Larger reunions that extend to an entire branch of the family will require a planning committee with a minimum of eight to ten volunteers meeting once a month for at least a year to plan the details. You'll need a large rented hall or outdoor park, a catered or potluck lunch or dinner, parking for a large number of cars, identification tags, activities for the children, prizes, multiple bathrooms, and directional maps for people who live some distance away. You may also need to have the guests pay a registration fee to cover the costs of the event, preferably collected ahead of time by mail. Large reunions often have one or more themes to attract family members.

Teaching Family History is a popular reunion theme and may include the sharing of photo albums, an ancestral wall of photos, a printed family tree, an oral and visual history presentation, or a bus trip to the original homestead and related buildings.

Something For Everyone! Is a reunion theme that attempts to be all-inclusive. Reunion planners can organize different activities by age groups. The youngsters might be involved in face-painting, water-balloon tossing, bubble blowing, or volleyball. Teenagers and adults may be involved in a baseball game, frisbee tossing, golf putting, and horseshoes.

Some reunions organize events sequentially, so that everyone watches the three-legged races or soccer game at the same time. A more elaborate method is to have several different events occur simultaneously to allow people to choose whichever events interest them.

Highlighting Family Talent is a third possible reunion theme. Several events are organized that require participants to demonstrate their musical, athletic, food preparation, or hobby craft talents. For example, a competition can be held for judging the best homemade jams or pies brought to the reunion by family members. Ribbons are awarded to the winners. If a stage area and sound system are available, a talent show can be organized comprised of singers, dancers, and people playing musical instruments.

For further information on organizing family reunions, you may wish to refer to one of the following books.

Family Reunion
by Jennifer Chrichton
Workman Publishing Co., 1998
ISBN 0761105859

A resource book of advice on planning various types of reunions from a one-day picnic to a week-long gathering. Topics include choosing a site, record keeping, entertaining kids, group activities, and gathering information on family history.

The Family Reunion Sourcebook
by Edith Wagner
McGraw-Hill Publishers, 1999
ISBN 0737301007

Written by the founder/editor of *Reunions* magazine, the book includes guidelines for ideal locations, meal planning, and group activities.

The Family Reunion Planner
by Donna Beasley and Donna Carter
Macmillan Publishers, 1997
ISBN 0028611934

Organizing large-scale reunions from an African-American perspective. A step-by-step handbook of creative ideas, activities, themes, and suggestions on managing the multitude of tasks for what many families regard as an annual pilgrimage.

Fun and Games for
Family Gatherings
by Adrienne Anderson
Betterway Books, 1996
ISBN 0961047054

An idea-generator containing 235 possible ways to entertain kids and teenagers at family reunions. Also includes listings of hotels and resorts across America that host reunion gatherings.

Project Two—Start a Social Activity Committee

If you live in an apartment building, retirement community, or housing project that contains several accommodations with retired couples or individuals, you
might consider organizing a "social activity committee."
This would be a small group in the building that is
interested in bringing people of the same age together
to pursue common interests.

Talk to people individually to drum up interest when
you meet them in the laundry room or in the hallways.
Invite two or three individuals to your place for coffee,
tea, and cake to discuss the idea. Suggest that it might
be possible to organize a weekly or monthly activity
for a group of retirees to bring them together and enjoy
each other's company. Activities might include a bingo
night, a bowling league, casino excursions, one-day
bus tours to see the sights, a dart competition, a card
playing night, an evening dining out, a catered buffet,
a costume party to celebrate Halloween, a group party
to celebrate New Year's Eve, a book review group, a
trip-sharing presentation night, or a hobby-sharing
afternoon.

Even the social activity planning meetings of the
committee can become a social event that gets people
together, with each of the members taking turns playing
host.

Talk to the rental manager and the building superintendent to get their approval and assistance. Many
buildings have a bulletin board for posting signs, often in the laundry room. Ask permission to post activity schedules. Many buildings have large unused storage

areas that might be converted into senior activity rooms for darts, cards, or the sale of handicrafts or the sale of baked goods. The money from the fund raisers can be reinvested in paint, chairs, and rugs to improve the activity room and make it more cheerful, or to subsidize upcoming events.

If you have organizational skills and enjoy the company of people your own age, this is a synergistic project that can be socially rewarding with new friendships, great company, and fun outings. It will brighten your perspective on your neighbors and the building in which you live. But this will all take time. It may take a year or more to get the committee active and the retiree population responsive. To get projects organized, work with the most outgoing and cheerful people in your community. Experiment with simple, inexpensive gatherings at first. Be encouraging, cheerful, persistent, and above all be patient with people.

Project Three—Teach a Hobby Course

Most people have at least one or more sets of skills that they are good at. These skills may be related to their favorite hobbies, the operation of a busy home, or the running of a business, they may be specific skills developed while working full time. Examples include gourmet and ethnic cooking, home repair, flower and vegetable gardening, computer installation skills, computer application skills, family history research, photography, videography, and oil painting. You probably can think of two or three additional skills not mentioned here. A number of these "hobby skills" have become the topics of popular television shows. People find them interesting and want to learn more about them.

You may have attended classes, workshops, or conferences to develop your expertise in a particular area. Once you have accumulated a body of knowledge on a topic and have some related skills to put the knowledge into practice, you can share that with others. One possibility you might consider is organizing and teaching a hobby course to retirees in the apartment building, retirement community, or housing project in which you live. Teaching the course in your apartment (with the permission of the building rental manager and/or superintendent) will eliminate the need for a rented classroom. You may choose to charge a nominal fee for your time and materials, or you may choose to teach it free of charge and enjoy the people's company as a reward. You can make it a social activity as well as a learning opportunity for retirees by offering a short coffee or tea break and a chance for people to chat in between the short lessons.

Market and present the course in a professional and congenial manner.

Preparation for teaching a hobby course involves several steps. First, you will need to decide the content of the course. What theoretical knowledge is involved? What skills need practicing? Second, how can this set of skills and body of knowledge be divided into a sequential set of individual lessons and spread over the number of workshops that you plan to present? Third, what teaching tools will you need? Will you need an erasable marker board or flip chart? Will you need extra chairs? Will you need plastic covering or newspapers for the floor (for painting sessions)? Will you need a videotape machine and a television set? Will you need a coffee percolator? Do you have access to a photocopier? Fourth, what is the best and most professional method of advertising the course to reach your intended audience?

This project requires organizational, teaching, and people skills from the instructor and can be rewarding financially and socially as well as increasing your self-esteem.

Preparing to Teach a Hobby Course

1. Make a list of topics to be taught.

2. Organize the topics into a sequence of four or five individual lessons.

3. Make a list of the materials, furniture, and equipment that will be required.

4. Find a space to offer the course.

5. Design and print professional-looking posters and/or brochures to advertise the course.

Project Four—Plan a Group Trip

One of the favorite pastimes of most retirees is traveling. People finally have the time and money to enjoy a leisurely vacation to some enjoyable destination. If you have a small or large group of friends, or if you belong to an association or collection of people who share common interests, you might consider organizing a trip for the entire group. This might be as simple as getting together a car convoy or a motorhome vacation with another couple, or signing up a group of people for a preselected escorted bus tour or cross-country train trip. On a more challenging level, you might consider planning and organizing the travel and lodging details of a group trip to some exotic resort where people could swim, play golf, hike and tennis.

Escorted tours are those in which the traveling, lodging reservations, and sightseeing destinations are handled by the travel company escort who accompanies the group on the trip. This person often caters to the needs of the individuals on the trip as well as acting as a tour guide by explaining historical facts and pointing out interesting sites. Escorted tours occur via several modes of transport including buses, trains, and cruise lines, and are popular in Europe as well as North America. If you prefer the trip's details to be handled by someone else, look for this escort tour option.

Trips with a theme are also popular, such as a golfing holiday for the group to some sunny destination with palm trees. Relatives might enjoy a return trip to the "old country" where their ancestors originated as part of a family history tour. Others might enjoy an ecological sightseeing tour along coastal waterways to watch whales, porpoises, or majestic glacial cliffs falling into the sea. Some others might like a country music trip to Brandon, Missouri, or to Nashville, Tennessee, to watch their favorite entertainers. Most cruise lines offer theme cruises with the onboard entertainment geared to a particular interest, such as jazz, gardening, sports and fitness, big band music, country music, or photography.

Unusual and fun vacations may be the type of trip that appeals to a large number in your group. They may enjoy a festival or celebration, or an unusual mode of transport. The Mardi Gras celebration in New Orleans offers a colorful parade, lively music, Cajun cuisine, and all-night pubs. An excursion down the Mississippi on a Mark Twain-era paddlewheel steamer, with dinners and lodging included, offers a fanciful trip into simpler times in history. A leisurely cross-country train trip with dining car, bubble observation deck, and sleeping berths may rekindle old memories. A week of Broadway stage plays in New York City, or in London, combined with exclusive dinners and sightseeing may provide hours of enjoyment. What about a musical tour of Ireland or Scotland with singing, step-dancing, fiddling, and laughs?

For additional resources on trips for seniors, please refer to the following organizations.

Seniors Abroad
12533 Pacato Circle North
San Diego, California 92128
Phone: 619-485-1696

Specializes in arranging vacations for the mature traveler, with the emphasis on totally hassle-free enjoyable trips.

Grand Circle Traveler
347 Congress Street
Boston, Massachusetts 02110
Phone: 1-800-221-2610

Another great resource for the senior traveller. Offers a free booklet called "Going Abroad: Tips for the Mature Traveler."

Destinations on Tape
Website: www.ontape.com

This travel agency website has a large library of tourism travel videos by country (U.S.A., Canada, Europe, Africa) and by method of travel, including ocean cruises, rail tours, Mississippi River and American West paddlewheel tours as well as golf and spa resorts. Tapes are $7 each plus shipping and handling. Great way to research a trip.

White Star Tours
Website: www.cruise.com
Phone: 1-800-800-9552

This cruise booking agency offers a 10 percent discount off typical cruise prices. Ocean cruise themes include golf, football, jazz festivals, classic music, country music, health and fitness, and ecological themes. Mississippi paddle wheel cruises offer a dozen different themes.

Project Five—Have a Garage Sale

You have probably spent a lifetime accumulating toys, tools, glassware, trinkets, music cassettes, CDs, VHS movies, pocket books, table-top appliances, baby clothes, strollers, and car parts. They are gathering dust in the garage, tool shed, basement, attic, and spare bedroom. Maybe it's time to reduce the clutter and have a weekend garage sale, and raise a bit of money for your next vacation.

Garage sales work best on a sunny day in the spring, summer, or fall. They also have the greatest attendance on the weekends when people are out for a drive and have the time to browse flea markets, antique fairs, and particularly garage sales. Although the term "garage sale" suggests that a driveway is a popular venue for table displays of your items, front lawns and backyards can also be substituted. Areas facing the street get the most exposure to passing motorists. The farther off a main traffic thoroughfare you are, the greater the need for "Garage Sale" directional signs to help potential customers locate your home. If you plan to have regular garage sales, you might consider purchasing inexpensive reusable signs in the hardware store or office supply store. Placing an advertisement in a local newspaper also will draw in customers looking for bargains. The following is a list of basic items needed for an effective garage sale:

Checklist For a Garage Sale

1. Several long tables for displaying items. Possibilities include folding card tables, picnic tables, long planks stretched between two supports.

2. Strips of two-inch-wide masking tape or white Avery labels for pricing items for sale.

3. Tablecloths for making the display more attractive.

4. Parking area for the cars.

5. "Garage Sale" directional signs posted on strategic telephone poles at nearby corners. Advertisement in local newspaper.

6. Folding lawn chairs for sellers to sit on (label "Not for Sale").

Project Six—Remodel Your Retirement Home

Many long-time homeowners downsize their accommodations at retirement and move into smaller accommodations, such as an apartment, condominium,
or mobile home community. The most common reason is to convert the capital gains the home has accumulated into usable spending money for their retirement. Other reasons include freedom from household
chores, such as cutting the grass, shoveling snow and
annual maintenance and repairs.

But what if you don't need the extra money? What if
you're a homebody and enjoy the neighborhood, the
nearby store conveniences, and the beautiful view from
your kitchen or living room window? Then the obvious
choice of accommodation may be to keep your family
home as your retirement haven. If this is your choice,
you may need to consider doing some remodeling to
convert the house into spaces more suited to your
retirement.

Remodeling a home can achieve a number of goals, for
example, increasing functionality by creating more open
spaces, such as a bigger kitchen, or making the home
a cheerier place in which to live through the addition
of brighter light fixtures for the evening and access to
more natural light for breakfast. Typically, older homes
have small dreary kitchens, clusters of tiny rooms,
and old bathroom fixtures. Tackling any of these areas
will improve how you feel about your home and about
yourself.

Remodeling your home may include enlarging the view
to the backyard by adding a well-lit sunroom with large

sliding glass doors that lead out to a wooden back patio for barbecuing and hosting patio parties in the summertime. Or it may involve landscaping a large but unused backyard into clusters of beautiful flower beds, winding pathways, and appealing green spaces with various types of trees and hanging bird feeders.

The remodeling process has several steps. One is to decide what it is that you wish to do to make your home more beautiful and comfortable. The second step is to hire professional consultants, such as a bathroom specialist, a kitchen specialist, or a landscaper, and ask them to draw up possible scenarios for rebuilding those areas. Most professional consultants have computer programs that can draw and print alternative room layout plans or backyard plans for you to look at. This is much easier than attempting to visualize how it will look. They can also give you new ideas based on the latest building products and building methods available. For major renovations, you may wish to have an architect draw up a blueprint of how the house will look after the renovations. Then you can hire a building contractor to complete the project.

If this sounds like too expensive an approach to remodeling, perhaps you and your spouse have the expertise to complete the project yourselves. Or maybe you have a building contractor in the family. If not, it might be prudent to ask as many people as possible for advice. You may have friends who recently gone through remodeling who can offer some caveats and suggestions. Building supply stores have staff consultants with free advice, and specialized builders, such as bathroom consultants, who are willing to make an evaluation of your home for free or for a small fee.

If there is a home improvement convention coming up in your area, it may be worthwhile attending. All the specialists that you need will be there and willing to dispense free advice. Bring large photographs and exact room dimensions of the areas you are considering for remodeling and have them looked at during the discussions. They can give you cost estimations based on the information you provide. For additional ideas on remodeling, you may wish to refer to the following resources:

Kitchens That Work: The Practical
Guide to Creating a Great Kitchen
by Martin Edic and Richard Edic
Taunton Publishers, 1999
ISBN 1561583197

Illustrated book on redoing the social center of your home from a lifestyle perspective. Includes working with kitchen contractors and designing "physical space" for people. 300 color photos and illustrations.

Porches and Sunrooms: Your
Guide to Planning and Remodelling
by Better Homes and Gardens (Editor)
Better Homes and Gardens Books, 2000
ISBN 0696211017

A book about deciding what type of room is right for the house before calling in the builder or architect. Covers indoor and outdoor sunrooms and porches. 150 color photos.

Creative Retirement

A Portfolio of Unique Deck Ideas
by Cy De Cosse
Creative Publishing International, 1996
ISBN 0865739749

Expand your living space into your yard with single-level or multi-level decks. 150 color photos.

Finishing Basements and Attics:
Ideas for Expanding Your Living Space
by Black & Decker Home Improvement
Creative Publishing International, 2000
ISBN 0865735832

How to convert unfinished space in the basement or attic into customized living areas, such as home offices, home theaters, and space for other relatives. Three hundred color photographs and illustrations.

Project Seven—Plan an Extended Vacation

It may sound a bit redundant for a retired person to take a vacation, but it's really true. When working full time, vacations served as stress relief and as a reward for working hard. Retirees have different motives for planning an annual vacation. These include escaping the cold weather, visiting distant relatives, adding some excitement into an otherwise dreary retirement, seeing and learning new things, and experiencing new cultures.

Traveling and going on extended vacations is a popular pastime among retired couples, best friends, religious groups, golf partners, and traveling buddies. There is a recent trend toward more escorted tours, such as European bus tours, and packaged vacations, such as cruises and specialized holiday resorts, as well as the exploration of foreign cultures.

When planning an extended vacation, that is, one in which you will be away from home for several weeks or months, it's important to consider what elements of the vacation are most important to you. What do you value the most: relaxing in warm climates, being around relatives, being physically active, learning new things, experiencing new cultures, being catered to, living in posh surroundings, or roughing it in the wild? Design your vacation around the things you that you value the most, and you'll return home with memorable rewarding experiences. Book a holiday without some thought on what pleases you the most and you may return unrested and disappointed. Not all vacations are equal in satisfying the heart, even if they cost the same amount.

If being around relatives is important, you might plan a long summer trip with a trailer or motorhome to visit distant relatives in various locations around the country. Be sure to include in your planning some side trips to popular tourist attractions, such as Niagara Falls, the Grand Canyon, Las Vegas, Dollywood, Nashville, Branson, Disney World, or the Houston Space Center. Conversely, the vacation might become a cross-country adventure with the main goal being to experience the sights, with visits to relatives as secondary side trips.

Escorted bus tours are fun and relatively inexpensive getaways. These are special tour coaches with a friendly onboard tour guide dedicated to taking a prepaid group to some particular attraction. Such tours number in the tens of thousands each year. Popular domestic bus tour destinations include country and western music trips to Branson, Missouri, and Nashville, Tennessee; historical excursions to Gettysburg, Pennsylvania, or Washington, D.C.; nature trips to see the fall colors and mountain vistas; or visits to the traditional farms of German Mennonite or Pennsylvania Dutch communities. Check the weekend travel section of your local newspaper or ask a travel agent to send you brochures of additional trips that might be of interest.

European bus tours to the British Isles, France, Belgium, Germany, Italy, and Switzerland are more expensive because of the airfare, but a delight for history buffs and for those wanting to experience different cultures. The experienced onboard tour guides will explain the important features of the country-side, arrange your overnight accommodations, and suggest the best places to eat in each country. Bring your passport and be prepared for early morning departures.

A slightly more luxurious and expensive way to tour Europe is to take river cruises aboard a cruise ship. They travel the long interconnected waterways and stop at various cities along the route to allow passengers to spend day trips exploring the cities. In the evenings, passengers return to the ship for dining and for sleeping. Peter Deilmann Cruises is one highly rated company that specializes in upscale ships that cruise the European waterways, including the Danube and the Rhône. See your travel agent for brochures on European cruises.

If money is no object, why not consider an exotic ocean cruise? Sleep, eat, and be entertained aboard ship while enjoying shore excursions to exotic coastal cities such as Wellington, Hong Kong, Shanghai, Singapore, Tokyo, and Honolulu. Other popular overseas cruises include exploring the old historic cities of the Mediterranean, or the northern Scandinavian, Finnish, and Russian cities of the Baltic Sea.

If money is absolutely no object, the world's first ocean-going resort cruise ship called *The World* has only 110 multi-roomed designer apartments and an additional 88 guest suites aboard for friends should they happen to drop in for a visit. For a mere one million dollars, you can purchase your floating condo and have a place to drop into when the mood strikes you, provided you can find out where it is at that particular moment. It might be helpful to have your personal floating condo installed with an On-Star® global-positioning device.

Project Eight—Organize a Supper Club

If you like organizing events, and you enjoy good food and the company of friends, you might consider organizing a supper club. This is a group of three to four couples who take turns hosting a dinner periodically, such as once a month or to mark special annual holidays. A minimum requirement is to have a dining room table that seats six to eight people and creative participants who love cooking from scratch.

This culinary social event with its tasty dishes can be organized on a simple rotation schedule, with each couple agreeing to host the event in their turn. The host would be in charge of setting the menu and offering a minimum of four courses: appetizers, soup or salad, the entree, and dessert. The idea is to present a meal that differs from the previous meals and to have the entire meal support a delectable and inventive main course. Featured entrees could be game or unusual meats such as venison, deer, moose, buffalo, wild boar, lamb, pheasant, ostrich, Arctic char, or Pacific salmon, or the dishes may be organized around an ethnic cuisine, such as Italian, Greek, German, French, Chinese, Japanese, Thai, or Mexican. Themes could be determined by season, or by celebrating special holidays, such as Christmas, Hanukah, Valentine's Day, New Year's, and Halloween. Locations can also vary from moonlit patios, outdoor barbecues, poolside gatherings, indoor candlelit dining rooms. The dinners can be a theme event with table and food decorations complementing that night's specific theme. Groups that have been in existence for some time typically become highly creative as the familiar meals of turkey, chicken, and roasts of beef have come and gone. Hosts have been known to spend hours researching exotic cookbooks and interviewing local restaurant chefs, as well as chefs discovered on their travels to foreign countries, to obtain novel dinner menus.

Some groups use a computer to print the recipes of each elaborate dinner, and offer them as a gift to each gourmet couple. The recipes can then be collected in binders or scrapbooks to create a unique cookbook of memorable mouthwatering meals. The collection would also make a delightful cookbook to pass to the next generation of supper club enthusiasts.

Project Nine—Visit the Wonders of the World

Some retirees may prefer to have specific goals or tasks to accomplish during their wanderlust travels throughout the world. Visiting and photographing spectacular and unique sights on earth may provide a worthwhile odyssey. Since the goal for your series of adventures may involve multiple trips to exotic destinations located all over the globe, several years may be required.

Because only one of the Seven Wonders of the Ancient World is still intact (the Great Pyramids of Egypt), you may have to be content with visiting more recent wonders. There are two fascinating categories, the Architectural Wonders of the World and the Natural Wonders of the World.

Architectural Wonders of the World are those edifices that are man-made, but are so colossal or unique in design that they hold an enduring fascination for people. According to astronauts, the Great Wall of China is the only man-made structure visible by the naked eye from outer space. The Colosseum of Rome is another great architectural monument. It once sported gladiators fighting to their death and remains standing in the middle of a modern bustling city. While in Italy, you may want to photograph the Leaning Tower of Pisa. This famous round tower is being worked on by several engineers to keep it from tilting any farther. But, just in case they fail, having one of the last pictures of it still standing will prove to be a great conversation piece. The Great Pyramids of Giza, located in the desert sands of northern Africa, is a favorite cluster of tombs of the once powerful ancient Egyptian pharaohs. The world's most famous and most photographed man-made edifices are in the United States and France, namely the Statue of Liberty, standing guard in New York Harbor, and the romanticized Eiffel Tower in Paris. Other grand edifices include Gothic cathedrals in France, the Parthenon in Athens, the Hagin Sopha mosque in Istanbul, the Moorish palace and gardens called Alhambra located in Granada, the Cambodian temple ruins of Angkor Wat, and pre-Columbian pyramids in Mexico.

Natural Wonders of the World are those created by nature and they are both fascinating and beautiful to photograph. The awe-inspiring Grand Canyon in Arizona is one example of a natural wonder. Niagara Falls, best viewed from the Canadian side, delights millions of visitors each year. The Ayers Rock in Australia is the largest single stone on earth, and for some reason it's sitting all by itself in the middle of a dry flat plain. How did it get there? While in Australia, visit the Great Barrier Reef, the world's largest series of coral reefs, located on the northern Australian coast. The Meteor Crater in Arizona is one of the largest holes ever dug by an extra-terrestrial meteor and will give you an idea of the devastating power such interplanetary bodies have on this planet. To enhance the effect, natural-wonder seekers may wish to view the CD movies *Armageddon* or *Sudden Impact* before traveling to the crater's edge. There are several majestic mountains worth photographing, including Mount Everest in Nepal, the highest mountain in the world, the Matterhorn, an infamous peak in Europe with sheer cliffs favored by risk-taking mountain climbers, and Kilimanjaro, the African mountain made famous by the Ernest Hemingway's short story.

Travelers have two major ways of experiencing these unique and wondrous sights. One is to be an observer, to view them, to photograph them. The other is to be a participant of either the culture surrounding an architectural delight or the physical realties of the natural wonder. For example, while photographing the Leaning Tower of Pisa, find an outdoor café with a view of the tower, have lunch, and chat with the locals. Experience the culture and learn the history of the tower. Learn the true name of the Colosseum in Rome (Flavian Amphitheater). Watch the movie *The Gladiator* starring Russell Crowe to get a feel for the breadth of the Roman Empire, then take a tour inside the actual Colosseum where the final gladiatorial battle took place. The ancient stone walls will come alive with history. After photographing the pyramids in Northern Africa, take a ride on a camel to experience one of the earliest forms of human travel.

One example of being a participant in a natural wonder setting is to take a ride on the *Maiden of the Mist* tour boat to the edge of the Niagara Falls Gorge, feel the water's mist on your face and listen to the roar of the falls. Or while at the Grand Canyon, take a river trip down the Colorado River or a helicopter ride through the majestic canyon walls and feel the power of a river capable of cutting through solid rock. While at the Great Barrier Reef, snorkel, scuba dive, or use a glass-bottom excursion boat to view the schools of colorful tropical fish that make the reefs their home.

Some travelers may wish to include a trip to photograph the stone faces of four U.S. Presidents carved into Mount Rushmore in South Dakota. Not far from Mount Rushmore, the stone face of Crazy Horse, the Indian chief who defeated General George Custer at the Little Big Horn, is currently under construction near Custer, South Dakota.

Additional natural wonders of interest include Yellowstone National Park, which has more active geysers than anywhere else in the world, including "Old Faithful," along with the park's free-ranging buffalo, wolves, and deer, and finally the giant sequoia trees found in Sequoia National Park, including "General Sherman," the world's largest living organism.

If you travel extensively, you may wish to consider being part of the Travelers' Century Club, an elite travel group headquartered in Santa Monica, California, whose applicants must have visited one hundred or more countries (out of a total of 314 countries in the entire world) to be eligible for a membership.

Creative Retirement

Project Ten—House Swap

One inexpensive way to get an extended vacation is to swap your house with another family, either from another country or another part of North America. This is ideal for people who enjoy traveling and experiencing a new locale as if they were one of its residents. You can enjoy your stay without the cost of renting a hotel, motel, or condominium. Consider swapping with people with similar economic status, backgrounds, and furnishings to ensure reasonably comfortable surroundings.

With a home exchange, each party often agrees to arrange for the prepayment, or automatic bank account deduction of utility expenses such as electricity, cable TV, and telephone, so that the temporary tenant does not have to deal with them. Each might also agree to retain a weekly cleaning lady to keep the households intact. The exchangers pay for their own food, travel, and car expenses, but essentially live rent free. It takes about six months to a year or more to plan a swap, so give yourself plenty of lead time.

Advertisements for home swapping can be found in the classified section of retirement magazines. There are also home swap agencies that you can reach by mail, telephone, or the World Wide Web. Websites and printed catalogs provide photos of the homes along with descriptions of their interiors, location, and how close they are to amenities.

If you are comfortable with this type of arrangement, make sure that both parties have current passports. Overseas swaps may require a temporary visa. Beware that visa applications will ask for your health status and may screen out any potential candidates who may require possible hospitalization while in the host country. For additional information, refer to the following resources.

Vacation Exchange Club
Box 820
Haleiwa, Hawaii 96712

Over 5,000 homes are listed in 40 countries with about half in North America, Europe, Australia, and New Zealand. Annual published listing. Membership is $35.

HomeExchange.com
Box 30085
Santa Barbara, California 931130
Phone: 805-898-9660
Fax: 805-898-9199
Website: www.HomeExchange.com

An Internet-based agency that offers hospitality home exchanges, accommodations, and vacation rentals. Based in Santa Barbara, California, this upscale website offers color photos and descriptions of homes around the world. Database listing is $30 per year.

Seniors Vacation and Home Exchange
Website: www.seniorshomeexchange.com

The only home exchange website exclusively for the over-50 age group. They offer more than 900 vacation opportunities in over 30 countries. Site has real-time e-mail capabilities to discuss the venture with a potential partner.

Chapter Eight

Projects For the Creative Person

Creative people find the most enjoyment in life when they create, invent, or design something from scratch, or modify an existing item to make it better. The final product may be aesthetic, such as art, music, or poetry, or practical, such as a computer program, an architectural drawing, an invention, a book, or a new procedure for accomplishing some task. The process of mentally creating something new brings them pleasure. Check off the projects that you might be interested in.

Projects in This Chapter:	✔
1. Join a Theater for Seniors	☐
2. Redecorate and Refurbish	☐
3. Play a Musical Instrument	☐
4. Write a Family History Book	☐
5. Create Your Own Video/CD	☐
6. Become a Painter	☐
7. Restore Furniture	☐
8. Take Up Photography	☐
9. Design Your Own Website	☐
10. Try a Handicraft Hobby	☐

Project One—Join a Theater For Seniors

If you have some dramatic flair, theater background, or creative organizational skills, you might consider joining a theater group that puts on stage plays. The regular season of plays is often profit-oriented, and auditions tend to be competitive and demanding. If you don't mind playing the role of minor characters until your credentials are established, your efforts can be very rewarding. There is, however, an enjoyable alternative aimed at retirees that you might consider.

Many places have theater for seniors—fun skits with singing and dancing presented once a year by a volunteer group of retired people. It tends to be less competitive, more fun-oriented, and is restricted to people over a certain age.

Your contribution to the event can be one of several possible roles. You might be one of the stage actors, background dancers, or singers. You may help to build stage props or sew the costumes, look after the lighting or the sound system, or design, print, and circulate brochures and posters to advertise the event. There are many fun supporting roles both on the stage and behind the scenes that need to be filled to make the performance a success. Consider your own personal set of talents when offering your assistance to the organizational committee. To find out where these people meet locally, talk to people at the theater where plays are usually held, or watch advertisements on your local community TV channel.

The following resources are related to seniors on stage in North America.

Senior Theater Connections
1236 NE Siskiyou Street
Portland, Oregon 97212
Fax: 503-249-1137
E-mail: bonnie@teleport.com
Website: www.seniortheatre.com

A website in Portland, Oregon, that provides a national directory devoted to seniors in the performing arts in the United States and Canada. It can connect you to actors, acting groups, available jobs, and reference books.

Senior Theater Connections
by Bonnie L. Vorenberg
Artage Publications, 1999
ISBN 0966941209

The first national directory for seniors interested in the performing arts. This large-format glossy paperback lists the names, addresses, and descriptions of theater groups in the United States, Canada, and Europe. Provides advice for finding courses, initiating, expanding, and funding senior theater groups.

Seniors Acting Up
by Ted Fuller, Editor
Publisher: Pleasant Hill, 1996
ISBN 0964977605

A collection of humorous one-act plays and skits for people or organizations wishing to put on plays for older adults.

Project Two—Redecorate and Refurbish

Retirement means that you will be spending much more time at your home than ever before. Redecorate and refurbish your house, apartment, or condominium. Give it a make-over, so that you get the maximum enjoyment and comfort from your environment. Make it functional, practical, and cozy. Do you need a specific hobby room, such as a sewing room, a den for your computer, or new work benches and tool racks for the basement? If you enjoy flowers and the outdoors, maybe it's time you hired a professional landscaper. Maybe the sunroom needs new windows and screens, or the backyard needs a new patio with a couple of comfortable deck chairs. Perhaps the furnace needs replacing, or an air conditioner needs to be installed. Has any part of your home been bothering you over the past few years? Now is the time to make changes.

Refurbishing and redecorating may coincide with simplifying your lifestyle and getting rid of old clothes, worn furniture, two-decade-old reference books, cobweb-covered items in the attic, basement, or garage. It's a great time for having a garage sale and donating unwanted items to Goodwill or the Salvation Army. Then turn your attention to the best retirement uses of the spaces inside your home. Make place for your favorite hobbies. Make your living space bright, uncluttered, and cheerful.

Give some thought as to how you want your home to appear. Your home did not get into the state that it's in overnight. Neither will your improvements happen quickly. Carry out the changes over a two or three-year period. There's no rush. Try this suggested approach.

Plan of Attack

1. Simplify. Throw stuff out that you haven't used for a long period of time.

2. Reduce the clutter. Give yourself more living space by reducing the amount of excess furniture in your home.

3. Repair, upgrade, or replace all necessary items.

4. Redecorate and refurbish the inside. Use paint and wallpaper to make it bright and cheerful.

5. Enhance the outside of your home and the beauty of your yard.

For further information on decorating and refurbishing a home, please refer to the following resources:

Home Decorating for Dummies
by Patricia and Katharine McMillan
IDG Books Worldwide, 1992
ISBN 0764551078

Practical, money-saving suggestions on space planning, furniture selection, window treatments, and accessorizing your own home. Contains 30 full-color photographs.

The Ultimate Decorating Book
by Judy Spours
Collins & Brown, 1999
ISBN 1855857294

An all-color decorating guide for beginners with 1,000 decorating ideas for the living room, bedroom, and kitchen. Create an inviting mood with colors, patterns, soft furnishings, paint, and wallpaper.

Decorating Makeovers
by Better Homes and Gardens
Meredith Books, 2003
ISBN 0696214040

This book is filled with room-by-room suggestions on how to use existing furnishing to create comfortable welcoming spaces. Helps you to establish a focal point in the room and apply decorating principles.

The New Decorating Book
by Better Homes and Gardens

Meredith Books, 2001
ISBN 0696213818

Featuring more than 500 full-color photographs of room treatments, this thorough manual discusses style, budgeting, color schemes, furniture fabrics, patterns, and seasonal make-makeovers.

Project Three—Play a Musical Instrument

Have you ever wished to play a musical instrument, such as the piano, electric keyboard, or guitar? Did you give up trying earlier in life because of the difficulty of reading music? Times have changed and so have musical instruments and the variety of methods for learning them.

You can take lessons by going to summer camp for musicians, listening to progressive audiotapes, watching television videos, or hiring a tutor. There are training methods for people who "learn by ear," as well as by traditional "sight reading" of notes.

Musical instruments have advanced with the adaptation of computer chips and audio circuit boards. The traditional acoustic piano now competes with the digital keyboard pianos to provide a range of piano sounds including grand concert, upright grands, Fender Rhodes piano, honky-tonk piano, and harpsichord. Music that you create can be saved on computer disk for later playback. Digital pianos can be purchased as portable stage models, or in attractive, enclosed wood-finish upright models as well as beautiful open-top grand piano models for the home, and they do not go out of tune. Several companies produce digital pianos including Kurzweil, Technics, and Yamaha.

The more musically sophisticated may prefer ensemble keyboard pianos, which can imitate other musical instruments for accompaniment such as drums, woodwind, and string instruments, and are also capable of creating multiple special effects, such as reverb and tremolo. You can also include disk storage for building your musical creations one layer at a time, by concentrating on the foreground and background instruments separately, like a multiple-tracked recording. Technics Corporation, the current leader in 88-key ensemble keyboards, can produce up to one thousand different sounds and interact with a user-friendly display screen. This fun instrument can make one person sound like a whole band or orchestra and warm the heart of even the most sophisticated player.

The traditional guitar has given way to multiple models—acoustic, electric acoustic, semi-hollow electrics, hard-body electric, and guitars with built-in synthesizing capabilities. Guitar players can now sound like a piano player, and a piano player can now sound like a guitar player. Both can sound like a violin. It depends on whether you prefer to tap keys or pluck strings to make the sound. There are even electronic drum kits available that imitate other instruments. Just think, you could tap a nice piano solo on your drums. The following information may prove helpful in your pursuit of piano or guitar training.

Amazing Secrets of Exciting Piano Playing
Website: www.playpiano.com

This excellent website, hosted by piano instructor Duane Shinn, offers both traditional and non-traditional methods for learning to play piano, including sheet music, audio cassette, and video cassette. Hundreds of courses are offered including pop, western, and gospel styles, using left-hand chords, fancy lead-ins and endings, improvision, and changing rhythms. Mail order courses available for both beginners and advanced-level piano players.

Encyclopedia of Picture Chords
by Leonard Vogler
Amsco Publications.
ISBN 0825615038

A keyboard reference book for piano and electronic keyboard players that uses photos of finger placements to illustrate how chords are formed on the keyboard.

National Guitar Workshops
Box 222
Lakeside, Connecticut 06758
Phone: 1-800-234-6479
e-mail: ngsw@esslink.com
Website: www.guitarworkshop.com

A series of week-long summer workshops for those in-terested in learning guitar, drums, or the keyboard. Well-organized sessions including theory and hands-on practice at three levels of difficulty with a typical faculty of 15 instructors. Operates in Connecticut, Tennessee, Washington, and California. Brochure available upon request. Fees include accommodation, courses, and meals—$900 US funds.

Guitar Workshops Plus
www.guitarworkshopplus.com
Operates summer guitar, keyboard, drum workshops in Oakville, Ontario, formerly National Guitar (above).

The Hot Licks Newsletter
Box 337
Pound Ridge, New York 10576
Phone: 914-763-8013 or 1-800-388-3008

A mail order catalog which lists descriptions and prices of musical instruction audiotapes, videotapes, books, and CDs for guitar.

Project Four—Write a Family History Book

One project that will be appreciated for years or even generations after its completion—is a book on your family history. This is a researched story about your ancestors your parents, grandparents, and great-grandparents—where they lived, where they went to school, their occupations, their living conditions, and what it was like in their respective communities.

The scope of the project will depend on the number of generations that you wish to present. The further back into the past you intend your book to go, the more in-depth research will be required. You may find it easier to follow just the family surname, instead of concentrating on both the paternal and maternal sides of the family. But remember to document both spouses in each nuclear family.

There are two basic types of research that family history writers use to uncover previous generations. The first type is referred to as oral history research and involves interviewing older living relatives. In addition to facts, such as birth dates and locations, personal interviews can bring out stories about what it was like to live fifty or seventy-five years ago, as well as the personalities and habits of relatives that they knew. These anecdotes can bring interest and color to an otherwise dull but necessary factual history of birth, marriage, and death dates. You can also talk to these people by phone or by writing letters, but those methods often yield much less information. Writing letters is the slowest research method. People often respond to letters as much as six months later, and letters requesting information usually generate about a ten percent rate of returns, particularly among those who are relative strangers.

The second type of investigation is referred to as archival research. This involves the use of government-run national archives, state or provincial archives, public libraries, and family history centers to uncover vital statistics (census data, births, marriage and death registrations) through national census data and church parish records. Such information is usually recorded on microfilm and will require that you learn to use a machine called a microfilm reader.

Archival research also involves researching non-government sources of information such as cemetery headstones, family Bibles with births, marriages, and deaths recorded in the center or at the back of the book, history books on the area in which they lived, obituaries found in past issues of local newspapers on microfilm, and memoirs or diaries in which relatives recorded personal family history.

One strong component of the family history book should be photographs of your ancestors, which you can scan into a computer, edit to remove unwanted features, such as borders, and then paste into your word processing document to accompany relatives' biographies. Most word processors have a "text box" or paragraph feature in the graphics menu that allows you to create a photo caption underneath each photograph to explain who is in the picture, and where and when it was taken. In addition to interviewing relatives, ask to borrow photographs for thirty days to get them copied, and then return the originals along with a thank you letter for the loan of the photographs and for their hospitality during the interview.

If you require additional literature on researching and writing family histories, you may wish to refer to the following references.

The Complete Idiot's Guide to Genealogy
by Christine Rose and Kay Germain Ingalls
Alpha Books 1997
ISBN 0028619471

Easy-to-read, humorous introduction to the hobby of researching family trees.

Writing Family Histories and Memoirs
by Kirk Polk
Betterway Books, 1995
ISBN 1558703942

Excellent book for beginning writers of family history books. Uses examples of writing styles and typical sample chapters. Highly recommended.

Project Five—Create Your Own Video/DVD

If you enjoy photography, and videography in particular, you might consider creating a video documentary on some topic complete with title credits, sound, and voice-over commentary. Topics might include your family on vacation, a family history, a self-help instructional video on some hobby, or a travelogue about your favorite town, place, or country. It could be a nature film concentrating on mammals, birds, fish, or insects. It could be a social commentary video on some controversial issue such as lifestyle changes, impact of clear-cutting in the logging industry, or the dumping of untreated waste water into our streams and lakes by industry and old city sewer systems. You can decide on your target audience—the people who will eventually view the video. Is it for private viewing among relatives and friends, or a television public service announcement, or an eventual commercial product for sale?

You will need several basic pieces of equipment. The best combination video system on the market is a digital video camcorder plus a colorful iMac Computer manufactured by Apple. The iMac with its friendly interface has specialized software called iMac DV for editing QuickTime scenes, adding music, sound effects, inserting titles, and utilizing some special effects, such as fade in and fade out. The software is designed for home use and is relatively easy to learn. Your camcorder hooks up to the computer with a single cable for transferring images. The final edited product then can be downloaded back to the camera for playback over its own viewing screen or viewed on your own television, converted to VHS videotape by plugging the camera cable into an input terminal in the back of a VHS machine or into the back of a DVD burner. The most popular storage format of iMac users is to place the completed digitized video into a service provider's free website with the help of the software. People can visit the website using their e-mail browser and watch the video.

Computers using Microsoft operating systems can install an easy-to-use consumer video editing software package called MGI Cinematic for $89.00 US. There are three separate packages for movie editing, each catering to the users' different levels of experience. For the novice, there is CineMagic (level one) which lets you choose a style—anything from a music video to an old-time movie—and the software assembles music, scenes, titles, and transitions automatically. Storybuilder (level two) guides you through the various choices step by step to assemble the movie. Advanced (level three) requires you to select all options on your own. The final product supports all popular output formats including video tape, DVDs, and Internet web page.

The Microsoft Windows XP operating system also contains a built-in video editor. It allows you to capture video sequences by plugging the camcorder into the back of the computer, then you can manipulate the video images frame by frame.

Producing a video or DVD requires the application of an array of artistic and technical skills. During its production, you will play the role of the scriptwriter, director, videographer, sound and lighting technician, and editor. It's a fascinating hobby for retirees with a creative side to their personality. For additional information on this hobby, refer to these resources.

The Film Maker's Home Page
Website: www.filmmaker.com

A resource website for artists involved in the production of various media, including film, DVDs, and videos.

How To Do Everything with Your iMac
by Todd Shauffer
McGraw-Hill Professional Publishing, 1999
ISBN 0072124164

Covers all things an iMac can do, including editing digital camcorder video clips.

The iMac for Dummies
by David Pogue
Hungry Minds, Inc., 1999
ISBN 07645064X

Excellent humorous book for absolute beginners. Starts with setting up the computer and operation of various software packages.

Project Six—Become a Painter

One hobby that combines creativity and artistic talent is painting. It's an absorbing personal hobby that can be done indoors or out with several possible sources of inspiration, including wildlife, wilderness scenes, still life, instructional workbooks, photographs, or live models, and can be accomplished from memory or from one's imagination. The finished works can decorate the walls of your home, or they can be sold or given away as gifts to family and friends. The most popular paint mediums are oil-based paints, acrylic paints, and watercolors.

Oil painting is the most traditional of the painting media. It gets its name from the paint medium that combines pigments (colors) with an oil base. One advantage is that you can paint over top of any mistake once the paint is dry. Oil-based pigments also remain constant while drying, so "what you see is what you get." One disadvantage of oil-based paints is that they take a day or two to dry before you can paint over top of previous scenes without smearing the colors together. They are also difficult to clean up. Brushes and paint and splatters on yourself and the floor need to be cleaned with a solvent, such as mineral spirits or turpentine. Murphy's Oil soap can be used to get spots out of clothing. Oil painting is done best on stretched canvas and with natural bristle brushes.

Acrylic painting is a more recently developed medium. It gets its name from the paint medium that combines pigments with a synthetic polymer binder. Brushes and paint splatters are easy to clean up with just soap and water. Acrylic paintings also dry within one hour and produce vivid colors, although not as glossy as in oil paintings. The disadvantage of acrylics is that pigments have a semi-opaque look before they dry, which makes it difficult to judge whether the image is going to turn out the way that you intended. Acrylic painting is best done on canvas, but also can be done on paper surfaces. Brushes labeled synthetic or nylon work best with acrylic paint.

Watercolor painting is the simplest medium to use. The artist dips the brush into a container of water and then onto the surface of solid, water-soluble pigment and then onto the paper surface. The advantages are ease of use, low cost, brushes and hands clean easily with water, and long-term storage of dry pigments. The disadvantage is that watercolor artwork can be easily damaged from water and high humidity.

Watercolors work best on any hard paper surface that can absorb pigment and water, but that do not wrinkle or shrink during the drying stage. Watercolor painting also works best with the paper flat on a table to prevent wet pigments from running.

The most expensive aspect of the hobby of painting is the framing of the final product, which often amounts to more than the combined cost of the paints, brushes, and canvas. An attractive frame and mat can often make the difference between an average-looking image and a sensational one.

To get started, it is recommended that you take a short course in oil, acrylic, or watercolor painting from experienced artists. They will provide the motivational support as well the artistic techniques necessary to achieve early successes. Other learning methods that provide excellent instruction include "how to paint" workbooks, websites on painting, and television shows that demonstrate various painting techniques.

Joy of Painting
by Bob Ross
Bob Ross Publications
Box 946
Sterling, Vermont 22170

A series of large-format instructional booklets based on his popular television show. Instructs reader on what color oil paints to purchase, and provides step-by-step illustrations for creating a particular painting.

Joy of Painting
Website: www.bobross.com
Bob Ross's website for purchasing instructional materials and supplies for oil painting.

Dorothy Dent Art
Website: www.ddent.com
Mail-order website for purchases of workbooks and instructional videos on scenic painting.

Fountain Studio/Graphics
Website: www.fountainstudio.com
Website for instructions and tips on watercolor painting by Ellen Fountain.

Project Seven—Restore Furniture

 If you are a handy person, you may enjoy furniture restoration. It's a hobby that provides a sense of personal satisfaction and may also prove profitable, if you use your skills to restore other people's furniture. Wooden antiques from garage sales, inherited living room or bedroom furniture from your parents or grandparents, or favorite but damaged furniture that you purchased during your lifetime, are usually common starting projects. They may include end tables, coffee tables, rocking chairs, hutches, bookcases, telephone stands, dresser drawers, or night tables. Typical damage may be discoloration, chipped surfaces, scratches, cigarette burns, coffee cup burns, broken legs, and missing hinges, latches, handles, or knobs.

Part of the secret of this type of hobby is owning a set of woodworking tools and machines, such as a drill, sander, and table saw, as well as having a knowledge of lacquers, varnishes, wood laminates, and lumber suitable for restoring broken furniture parts. This knowledge and skill development can be obtained from a number of sources. Local high schools and community colleges often offer hobby courses in furniture making and furniture restoration in the evenings during the winter. Check fall catalogues or phone the local school board and ask about extension or adult education courses in your area.

Another source of training may come from building supply centers, such as Home Depot, that offer short workshops to potential customers as well as how-to manuals on furniture restoration. Go down to the building center and ask the manager about learning opportunities.

A third source to learn the trade secrets is to read books that specialize in various aspects of the furniture restoration process. They usually come with step-by-step illustrations and photographs of various wood-repair projects, and they describe the tools and materials that you will need. These can be obtained at the bookstore in the hobby section, from Internet book sellers, and from building centers.

The minimum requirements will be different grades of sandpaper, a hand-held sander, one and two-inch brushes, wood putty, matching varnishes, sealers, and a workplace, such as the basement or the garage where the noise, smells of drying varnish, and powdered wood dust will not disturb other members of your family.

For further research, you may wish to consult the following sources:

The Complete Manual of Woodworking
by Jackson, Day, and Jennings
Knopf Publishers, 1997
ISBN 0679766111

A beautifully illustrated, comprehensive overview of the craft of woodworking. Topics include how to select hand tools, power tool maintenance, types of wood, instruction on woodworking techniques. Popular reference for beginners.

Refinishing Old Furniture
by Wagoner and Wagoner
Tab Books, 1995
ISBN   0830634967

An illustrated introductory guide to refinishing old and antique furniture. Takes readers through structural repairs and the process of restoring faded and damaged furniture.

Project Eight—Take Up Photography

If you enjoy taking pictures during holidays or on vacations, you might consider expanding your interest in the art of photography. This hobby has broadened significantly over the past decade with new inroads in camera technology and image processing, all of which make photography easier and more fun. There are now digital cameras that record images on thin memory modules as well as traditional cameras that record images on film. Digital cameras, although they easily connect to a pocket, laptop, or table model computer, tend to cost twice as much as a traditional camera. However, traditional photographs can also be scanned into a computer using a computer scanner to create a digital image.

There are several easy-to-use photo editing software packages for under $100, such as Picture It!, Photo Suite, and Photo Deluxe, that permit hobbyists to improve, enhance, or alter photographs. Capabilities include removing red eye, altering contrast, lightening or darkening, removing backgrounds, adding decorative frames, and placing phrases like "Happy Birthday" under the photograph to make a greeting card. There are also several inexpensive color printers specifically designed to print photographs on plain printer paper or special photographic paper. More expensive versions of the same software will permit more editing control, such as wrinkle and blemish removal in people's faces.

Digital computers have expanded what can be done with photographs. In the past, photo hobbyists had their film developed and typically placed the glossy prints in a scrapbook, photo album, or wall or desk frame. Now photo images can be e-mailed from one computer to another, made part of an electronic photo album, or inserted into a personal or business website. Camera shops will even put photos on coffee mugs or t-shirts to create personalized gifts.

There are three easy types of photography that hobbyists enjoy because they can combine them with other activities: travel, nature, and outdoor portrait photography.

Travel photography involves photographing people, architecture, and artifacts that you encounter on your vacations. This is primarily done to record memories of the trip and to share them with friends and relatives back home. Several travelers have created personal websites on their computer with titles such as "Egypt" and "Jungles of the Amazon" to display their photographic collection and to describe their trip to interested web surfers seeking information on those topics.

Nature photography is a broad term that includes most photography which is done outdoors with landscapes, animals, and plants as the central theme. Often, outdoor photographers concentrate on just one aspect of nature like beautiful scenes of rivers, mountains, and sunsets reflected on the water, or large mammals such as bears, deer, and moose, or various kinds of birds, or closeups of flowering plants.

Natural light portrait photography concentrates on photographing people, using only natural light from the sun. The photographs typically focus on the person's face or upper half of the person's body. The most flattering portraits can be taken in bright sunlight in the mornings between 9 A.M. and 11 A.M. and in the afternoons between and 1 A.M. and 3 P.M. When first experimenting with natural light portraits, it may be helpful to avoid taking portraits when the sun is directly overhead (around noon) because the sunlight creates unflattering shadows on the person's face. Also, photographs taken on cloudy days and near dusk generally result in poor- quality skin tones in the photographs. One secret to overcoming excessive shadows on a person's face is to use the camera's flash to fill in the poorly lit areas. This is particularly true when the sun is behind the subject which causes their face to be in shadow.

Be selective with your portfolio. Keep your best shots and discard the rest. Even professional and well-known photographers may only get a half dozen good shots out of an entire roll of film. If professionals put only their best pictures on display for people to see, why shouldn't you? For additional information on photography, you may wish to refer to the following guides.

How to Take Great
Photographs With Any Camera
by Jerry Hughes
Phillips Lane Publisher, 2001
ISBN 0963434896

Informative, uncomplicated guide for the wannabe photographer. Teaches creative photography with humor and simplicity.

Kodak Guide to Shooting Great Travel Pictures
by Jeff Wignall
Fodors Travel Publications, 2000
ISBN 0679032436

Full-color guide packed with easy tips and foolproof ideas for beginning travel photographers. In-depth look at portraits, landscapes, cityscapes, jungles, and rainy days.

National Geographic Photography
Field Guide: Secrets to Making Great Pictures
by Peter N. Burian, Robert Caputo
National Geographic Society, 1999
ISBN 0792274989

Excellent guide for beginning and intermediate photographers. Full of beautiful color photographs. Highly recommended.

Digital Photography! I Didn't
Know You Could Do That ...
by Erica Sadun
Sybex, 2000
ISBN 0782128432

For the novice photographer who owns a digital camera. Main topics include: transferring images from camera to computer and using Photo Deluxe software to edit images. CD-ROM software included.

Project Nine—Design Your Own Website

Retirees who have access to the Internet can design a personal website, market it, and allow web surfers to view it even when the home computer is turned off, all for free. This is a great way to share hobbies, expertise, ideas, and concepts with thousands of other people. Hobbies, such as genealogy, birding, sports, traveling, and gardening can be placed in the website. It can also be useful for advertising special events, such as an upcoming family reunion, anniversary, or homecoming, as well as a way of marketing stamp collections, coin collections, antique cars, musical talent, home vacation exchanges, and new ideas.

Most Internet providers, such as your local telephone or cable company, also allow subscribers to create their own personal website and store it on their host server computer, free of charge. Apple Computer Corporation has a similar hosting site for iMac video creations. The only limitation of the website is a preset limit to the storage space, such as five to ten megabytes. This will limit a personal website space to a maximum of five different screens of textual information. In addition, latest versions of major Internet browsers provide free design software, such as Netscape's Composer or Internet Explorer's Front Page Express, to do page layouts with text and graphics, and provide a way of transferring it from a personal computer to their new home on the host server.

Once the website address has been established, the designer can let other people know where it is by listing the address on the larger network portals, such as Yahoo and Alta Vista, by searching for the webmaster label and following the instructions for inserting new listings. You can leave several keyword phrases, such as "Williams Family Reunion" or "Tennessee Reunion," that web surfers might use as keywords to search for such information and locate that one specific website. This process is equivalent to listing your phone number in a telephone book.

People wishing to turn their home computer into a dedicated website server can design a personal website, then store the completed website on the server with its own dedicated modem and phone line. Internet surfers should be able to access the server twenty-four hours a day. This means that your computer must be on all the time. Typically, retirees with their own dedicated home server computer tend to use it to operate a small Internet business. To avoid the technical problems associated with a home server, many home businesses hire a website design business to design and host the website (keep the website on their server with twenty-four-hours-a-day access.) Website host companies charge $50-$100 per month for the service. Hobbyists, on the other hand, should use the free space provided by Internet providers. For additional information, you can refer to the following sources of information.

Easy Web Page Creation
by Mary Millhollen, Jeff Castrina
Microsoft Press, 2001
ISBN 0735611874

Nontechnical book for beginners who want to build their own home pages but don't know where to start. Uses color

Creative Retirement

photos of screens from Microsoft Word and Front Page Express.

Complete Idiot's Guide to Creating A Web Page
by Paul McFredries
Que Publishers, 1999
ISBN 0789722569

A book/CD guide that covers the entire process of web page design in a simple, friendly way. The CD contains HTML editors, graphics, and web pages.

Great Website Design Tips
Website: www.unplug.com/great/

Helpful website for web page designers. Includes free stuff, beginning tips, graphic tips, advanced tips, and expert tips.

Project Ten—Try a Handicraft Hobby

Creative people who love using their hands to create beautiful, unique objects should consider expanding their skills by taking community craft workshops or asking a friend to share their skills in a particular hobby. Handicrafts are created in almost any medium. Some are quite permanent, such as ornamental iron-work, concrete mouldings, and moulded brass ornaments, and some are quite transitory, like ice or food sculptures. There are three popular handicraft categories with easier media in which novice handicraft hobbyists can explore their creativity, namely, needlecraft artwork, woodworking, and stained glass making.

Needlecraft artwork is a general term that covers a variety of needlecraft projects, including crocheting and needlepoint. Crocheting refers to the construction of an ornamental mat of lace by working cotton, silk, or wool thread into patterns of intertwined loops with a hook. Sample projects include lace trim, end-table or chair-back doilies, lace tablecloths, dresses for antique dolls, afghans, and sweaters with decorative designs.

Needlepoint refers to fine embroidery created with a threaded needle, a starched cloth mesh held steady in a frame or a floor stand, and a variety of stitching techniques, the most popular of which is cross-stitching (makes an X pattern), but also includes continental stitching and basket-weave stitching. Popular threads include Persian wool, Medici French wool, and cotton embroidery floss. Sample needlepoint projects include cushion covers, chair covers, purse decorations, wall hangings, tapestries, heirloom designs, and framed artwork or quotations, like "Bless Our Home." Plastic canvas backing can be used to create more rigid, waterproof projects, such as dining table place mats and drink coasters. The artwork can be adapted from a photograph or picture, from a needlepoint book instructional chart, from prepainted or stamped canvas, or from one's imagination.

Woodworking is also a popular handicraft hobby. Favorite woodworking projects include bird houses, decorative doorknockers, mailboxes, key holders, tool racks, front lawn ornaments, wooden toy trucks and trains for young grandchildren, and home or cottage signs with carved lettering. A hand-held sander, power drill with wood cutting drill bits, and a small handsaw are the woodworker's tools, along with paint, stains, and wood glue. Wood carving requires a set of special chisels and softwood lumber.

Stained glass is a hobby craft that generates colorful translucent glass panel decorations of various shapes and designs that are hung in windows to catch the sunlight or used as panel inserts in windows and doors. The construction process includes glass cutting and grinding, copper foiling or lead trim, soldering, and forming glass sections into an overall shape, such as a circle, triangle, butterfly, or swan.

Enrolling in a workshop to learn the basic techniques is recommended. Stained glass kits can be purchased in hobby stores.

Handicrafts have a variety of uses in addition to brightening up one's home and property, including church or charity fund raising, revenue-generating craft sales, and special gifts for friends and relatives. For additional information on these hobbies, you can refer to the following books.

The Complete Needlepoint Guide:
400+ Needlepoint Stitches
by Susan Sturgeon-Roberts
Krause Publications, 2000
ISBN 0873417933

The definitive reference for the needlepoint artist. Suitable for beginners to advanced hobbyists. Includes 400 black and white photographs plus hundreds of stitch diagrams.

Splendid Needlepoint:
40 Beautiful and Distinctive Designs
by Catherine Reurs and Deborah Morgenthal
Lark Books, 1997
ISBN 1887374221

A practical, inspiring, user-friendly guide for creating forty projects with animal, floral, and holiday designs.

Birdhouses: 20 Unique Woodworking
Projects for Houses and Feeders
by Mark Ramuz and Frank Delicata
Storey Books, 1996
ISBN 0882669176

Easy-to-follow manual on birdhouse projects ranging from a simple cabin to a Gothic castle. Projects are organized from simplest to the most difficult.

Stained Glass Basics: Techniques, Tools, Projects
by Rich, Mitchell, and Ward
Sterling Publications, 1997
ISBN 0806948779

Creative Retirement

Simple stained glass projects of varying sizes selected for the beginner. Projects include panels, boxes, and lampshades.

Chapter Nine

Projects For the Socializer

The social person tends to seek out the company of others to find happiness. This may include close relatives, personal friends, or organizational and institutional groups that share common interests. This chapter provides ten creative suggestions for a retired socializer who enjoys mingling with people around some collective theme. Check off the projects that you might be interested in.

Projects in This Chapter:	✔
1. Join a Retirement Community	☐
2. Find a Soul Mate	☐
3. Host a Weekly Card Party	☐
4. Join a Bowling League	☐
5. Join a Church Auxiliary	☐
6. Try an Internet Chat Room	☐
7. Go Cruising	☐
8. Take the Grandchildren on Vacation	☐
9. Join a Seniors' Activity Center	☐
10. Do Something Entirely Different	☐

Project One—Join a Retirement Community

If you enjoy the company of people your own age and like having a variety of social events to attend, you might consider becoming a member of a retirement community that is specifically designed for independent, healthy seniors. There are two basic types: enclosed housing communities and condominium high rises.

Enclosed housing communities include landscaped streets of bungalow homes, semidetached condominiums, or the less expensive but equally as comfortable mobile home retirement parks. These are favorite locations for couples who enjoy having a plot of land of their own, a lawn to mow, a flower garden to plant, and a building to look after. These private enclosed communities have their own roads, street lights, and sidewalks. They also share a common community center with daily activities like aerobics, craft lessons, woodworking, or oil painting, and activities like bingo, line dancing, square dancing, round dancing, clogging, movie nights, live theatre, cribbage, bridge, hearts tournaments, and dart leagues. Some have access to a swimming pool or a nearby golf course. These communities often have minimum age restrictions, usually fifty-five, and generally do not favor young families.

Condominium high-rises, the second category of retirement accommodations, are well-suited to single individuals or to those retirees with some physical disabilities. There is no building maintenance to worry about, such as cutting the grass, raking leaves, or shoveling snow. The one or two-bedroom apartments are purchased by the retirees and can be modified to suit the owner's decorating tastes. The multi-story building will typically have shared community facilities like a swimming pool, a game room, and a large banquet/activity room. Often a park with walking trails or a golf course will be located nearby. Sample activities include local craft sales, bingo, card tournaments, ethnic food nights, swimming, water exercise classes, aerobics, and dance nights.

The great advantage of these living environments is that your social life is handed to you on a silver platter. There will be a constant flow of daily or weekly activities in which to participate, and people your own age to associate and celebrate special events with, like Halloween or New Year's Eve. You can select which activities to attend, and then you can fill in the rest of your time with your other hobbies and pastimes.

Often retirees will seek communities with people of similar backgrounds. Some communities may contain a concentration of retirees only, seasonal residents, people of a particular religious group, people who speak a second language, or people from a similar part of the country. Find one in which you can feel comfortable.

A second major criterion for selecting a retirement community is the location. Many North American towns and cities have built retirement living centers and may promote their entire town as a retirement community to attract retirees from across the country. If you enjoy the year-round climate of your particular area, and want to remain close to your children and grandchildren, consider calling for brochures. Local newspapers and retirement magazines often contain advertisements for these retirement communities.

You may also wish to consider purchasing ownership or long-term rental of facilities in a southern climate retirement community to use strictly as a winter resort. Your regular home then becomes your summer resort. Retirees that do this are often referred to as "snowbirds" because they tend to head south before the snow arrives in their hometown. Florida, Arizona, Texas, California, Mexico, and Costa Rica are popular destinations.

A word of caution is necessary. Be sure to do your research before making a major lifestyle move. Try out the prospective property on a trial basis to see if you enjoy the change in lifestyle. Instead of selling your own home immediately, consider renting it to a quiet couple for a year while you test the new lifestyle. This way, your bridges are not burned if you decide to return to your home. For additional information, you may wish to refer to the following reference material.

Retirement Communities Website
Website: www.eldernet.com

This Eldernet website provides links to retirement resorts and retirement communities located throughout the United States.

Retirement Places Rated
by David Savageau
Hungry Minds, Inc., 1995
ISBN 0028620844

Popular reference that rates 200 towns and communities in the United States by specific criteria such as cost of living, housing, climate, restaurants, movie theatres, libraries, and personal safety.

America's 100 Best Places to Retire
by Richard L. Fox (Editor)
Vacation Publications, 2000
ISBN   0964421674

In-depth profiles of 100 best cities and towns for active retirements. Grouped in categories of Ten Best: seaside, college towns, mountain communities.

50 Fabulous Planned Retirement
Communities for Active Adults
 by Robert Greenwald
Career Press, 1998
ISBN 1564143473

The fifty best master-planned retirement communities in the United States designed for people with an active lifestyle. Typical facilities in these communities include walking trails, gyms, swimming pools, and courses offered to seniors at a nearby college.

Project Two—Find a Soul Mate

About 40 percent of all North Americans over the age of sixty are single, widowed, separated or divorced. So at a stage in life when they have the time to share extended vacations, attend live theatre, go to movies, or take walks along the beach, suddenly there may be no one to share these activities with.

The need for love and companionship are two of the strongest emotional requirements of human beings. Both reaffirm our presence and validity in the world. Both give us a sense of fulfilment and completion as people. But if "love makes the world go around," how do you go about finding a soul mate?

Most people at this age are past the traditional bar scene. But there are some institutional venues, such as singles dances and socials put on by churches or associations, wine-tasting clubs, and gourmet dining clubs that encourage mixing among a group of people with similar interests.

An increasingly popular alternative approach to meeting people is to advertise. You might consider placing an ad in retirement magazines or your local newspaper under "companions." An honest, well-phrased advertisement that describes yourself, your interests, and the age and type of companion that you are seeking may elicit several fascinating responses worth pursuing.

There are a number of agencies that provide ways to contact possible companions. Several Internet websites provide a companion-finding service. The websites are usually free to browse and/or to submit a listing, but charge a small fee for any contacts that you initiate. Online services have the advantage of being able to scan potential dates by region, age, and range of interests. They usually have the capabilities of including a photo to accompany the person's profile. Other services include chat lines and newsletters. Two such web service companies are Webpersonals.com and Oneandonly.com.

Webpersonals.com is a singles service website for men and women. The company offers biographies, photos, and selective searching of their database and charges fifteen dollars for a number of contacts. It's an easy-to-navigate website offering three choices of companionship: casual dating, romance, and intimate sexual relationships. The company also offers "telepersonals," which are voice messages left in their database. You can also take an "escorted tour" with Kathy as she explains the various features of the website.

Oneandonly.com boasts over 250,000 ads and about 88,000 responses in a given week. The site offers biographies and photos of participants and database searches by geographic location, age, physical characteristics, lifestyle, or based just on photos. Both browsing and posting a listing are free, but a small fee is charged for contacts.

The photos and search capabilities of these enormous databases are definite assets for the anyone searching for a companion. The disadvantage is that there may not be anyone in your particular city or region in the database. The larger the city, the better chance of a match. If you live in a small community, local newspapers or regional companion services may be a better choice.

One and Only Personals
Website: www.oneandonly.com
Singles website for men and women. Allows database searches by five different criteria. Browse for free.

Webpersonals
Website: www.webpersonals.com
Easy-to-navigate website for singles. Offers three choices of relationships. Browse for free. Contacts: $15/each.

Dating for Dummies
by Joy Brown
IDG Books Worldwide 1997
ISBN 0764550721

Dr. Joy Brown, a clinical psychologist and talk show host, offers a funny, well-written book on the art of dating. Includes tips on when you are ready, where to find someone, and how to handle the first few dates. Also available on audiocassette.

Single No More: How and Where
to Meet Your Perfect Mate
by Ellen Kreidman
Renaissance Books, 2000
ISBN 1580631495

Practical, no-nonsense approach to dating by the author of several books. Helps you to identify, before you go on your first date, whether that person is the kind of individual you'd want to fall in love with. Also available on audiocassette.

Project Three—Host a Weekly Card Party

One way to get a foursome together on a regular basis is to organize a gathering of friends to play cards. The activity itself can be a great social event among the participants by having some light finger foods, and tea or coffee and inviting conversation about families and lifestyles. By being the first host, the organizer can ensure that the activity gets off to a good start. The original host may suggest that each participant, in turn, hosts the event, which lessens the pressure on any one household always being responsible for the food preparation and cleaning up after the event.

The choice of what card game to play is also important. Some card games lend themselves to intense competition between the players, and perhaps to potential personality conflicts. Betting money may also increase tension between the players. Typical competitive card games include poker and bridge. Some less competitive card games include hearts, rummy, and cribbage.

Mixed-gender card parties often become evening social events as an after-dinner activity. Single-gender card parties may work best in the early afternoon, from 1 P.M. to 3 P.M. Participants will have to decide whether the game is a smoking or non-smoking event.

In the final analysis, the success of a card party is usually determined by the personalities of the participants. If you wish to have a fun time, choose people who are good-natured, who like conversing, and who are fun to be around. They make the best friends.

According to Hoyle: Official Rules to More
Than 200 Popular Games of Skill and Chance
by Richard L. Frey
Fawcette Books, 1998
ISBN 0449211126

Complete set of rules and advice for winning at card games, dice games, parlor games, chess, checkers, and backgammon.

Barefoot Contessa Parties!
Recipes That Are Really Fun
by Ina Garten and James Merrell
Clarkson Potter Publishers, 2001
ISBN 0609606441

Well-thought-out party planner with ideas and a collection of entertaining theme parties from pizza to hors d'oeuvres. Includes ideas for drinks, coffee, venues, creating atmosphere, table decorations, and party surprises. Food recipes and photos included.
Hardcover, 264 pages.

Project Four—Join a Bowling League

One wholesome social activity that combines some exercise with group conversations is league bowling. It ranks second to soccer as the most popular participant game in the world. Joining a league, rather than random bowling, ensures that the social outing becomes a weekly event and that you get to know and chat with your teammates on a regular basis. The dress code is casual, and the competition between team members or other teams tends to be friendly rather than aggressive. Special bowling shoes are required to prevent alley damage and they can be rented at the main desk.

There are two variations of bowling in North America. One is called five-pin bowling, or sometimes Canadian five-pin, in which a 3.5 lb. bowling ball that fits in the palm of your hand is rolled down the alley at five smaller-sized pins. Ten-pin bowling is a version in which the participant uses a three-fingered grip on a 16-lb. ball and attempts to knock down of ten larger-sized pins. Both use the same length of bowling lane. Ten-pin bowling is by far the more popular version of the sport throughout North America. Although Canada has both versions, about 500,000 people are active five-pin bowlers and this version is particularly popular among youngsters and seniors because of the lighter-weight bowling ball.

League bowling organizes several teams to play against each other simultaneously using adjacent alleys. There are men's and women's bowling leagues, mixed bowling leagues, and senior bowling leagues, which allows you the option of choosing the group in which you will feel most comfortable. Senior leagues often play in the morning or early afternoon, while the others tend to play in the evenings (after work).

Often times, league bowlers will bowl one, two, or three games during an outing, An entire game might take thirty to forty-five minutes, depending on the number of participants on your team. The whole afternoon or evening, including getting coffee or a soft drink, may be one and a half to two hours in length. A phone call to a local bowling alley will inform you on what leagues and lane times are available.

Bowler's Start-Up: A Beginner's Guide to Bowling
by Doug Werner
Track Publishers, 1995
ISBN   18884654053

This beginner's bowling guide provides a basic reference to the sport. Written with wit and humor, this inexpensive little book will put those pesky bowling pins back in perspective. Black and white photographs.

Project Five—Join a Church Auxiliary

All churches, synagogues, and mosques have behind-the-scenes support groups that perform various functions, such as administrative, financial, fund raising, and social events coordination. If you wish to be involved in the social aspects of the church or other religious institution, you might consider joining either the fundraising group or the one designated the "church social" group. Each religious institution has different names for these entities, but the groups will perform similar functions.

The fund raising group, as the name implies, is in charge of raising monies for church use, in addition to the collections raised during the church service. Often, fund raisers are targeted at specific projects, such as operating a summer camp for kids, helping an economically distressed parishioner, purchasing a new church organ, or replacing worn furniture and equipment. The group's fund raising methods may include bingo nights, a bake sale, a penny table (selling donated items), a special events dinner, or selling greeting cards.

The social activity group concentrates on making sure that coming to church becomes a social outing as well as a religious experience. This helps to bond the members of the church. This group might operate a tiny-tot nursery while the services are going on, or provide tea, coffee, and cake immediately after the service for parishioners who choose to stay and chat. This group may also put on special social evenings in the church basement, like a play presented by the pre-teens in the congregation or even during the religious service. They may organize a summer church picnic.

Generally, the majority of the members of the social and fund raising groups are women, but often men will join in and be asked to perform tasks like setting up tables, using the ladder to hang decorations, kitchen duties, and cleanup. If you are interested in a social outing with people who are altruistic and kind hearted, and you have specific skills to offer, such as cooking, making crafts, display or marketing skills, or fund raising experience, inquire at your local church.

Website Keywords: Volunteering at Church

People seeking additional ideas for volunteering in your community through your local church should look through what other church websites have posted on the Internet. Many offer a wide range of caregiving activities and volunteer services.

Project Six—Try an Internet Chat Room

If you are a wee bit shy and do not mind using a computer, one way to keep in contact with people your own age is to get in on an Internet chat room. It's a nonthreatening way to meet people and possibly develop an Internet pen pal or even a lifelong friend. You should have no problem finding others of a similar inclination because, after teenagers, retirees are the next largest group of chat room users in North America. Retirees are generally daytime users.

Internet chat rooms are website "common rooms" for conversing with other people who are also seeking someone to chat with on a particular day. Most users register with the website and give a user ID that will appear before your comments in the chat room. People tend to use simple IDs such as "Bert," "Perky," "Grumpy," "Sagittarius," or message-related handles such as "Seeking Help," or "All-Thumbs." You can be as forthright or as anonymous as you wish, depending on your need for privacy. Chat rooms usually ask for your town of residence to help other users.

Chat rooms are not private. Anyone signed on to that particular chat room can follow along or join in with the conversations already in progress. Most chat rooms have a sidebar listing of people "sitting" in the chat room with you. If no one is in there, a computer message will say, "No one is in the chat room at this moment."

Chat rooms are spontaneous, interactive, and can be helpful if you are seeking help with some task or decision. Many chat rooms have topic-directed discussion forums that predefine the main topic of conversation. They also have rules of use and etiquette to govern behavior. Within those boundaries, the experience is similar to being in a living room during a party. People just come over and start a conversation.

What you talk about is often determined by the website you choose to enter. Preselected topics are usually the trend at retiree websites, such as those at the American Association of Retired Persons and the Canadian Association of Retired Persons. The AARP website has a discussion center with interactive bulletin boards where you can post your thoughts, experiences, or questions. Some of the topics in the discussion center include book talk, favorite computer links, travel stories, history discussions, and "about your life."

CARP has an imaginative, easy-to-navigate website listed under the "Fifty-Plus" banner. Their discussion forums are found in "The Back Fence" section of the main page and are billed as a virtual community center with sixteen discussion topics, greeting cards, daily horoscopes, and fun activities.

Senior.com is a website that advertises itself as 'The Best Online Community For Seniors." In addition to offering a wide range of articles, medical advice, and entertainment, it also has twenty-one forums (topic-specific chat rooms) and two additional general chat rooms that bring together seniors from around the English-speaking world. So, if you prefer an interesting chat with someone from Australia or Europe as well as urban and rural America, try that site.

American Association of Retired Persons
Website: www.AARP.org

Canadian Association of Retired Persons
Website: www.fifty-plus.net

Senior.com
Website: www.senior.com

Project Seven—Go Cruising

Retirees who like to meet people and travel to exotic places and are not hindered by finances may find ocean cruises very appealing. Cruising is the only type of holiday where the mode of transportation becomes as important as the destination. Essentially you are booking five things simultaneously with a cruise line— transportation, hotel reservations, dining reservations, entertainment, and a great social environment for meeting people, including bars, karaoke, dancing, and swimming. Quite often half the people on board are repeat cruisers, some averaging two cruises per year, one in the summer and one in the winter.

Cruises are not only popular vacation formats, but also great gathering places for people who are retired. These huge floating hotels provide your meals (four per day), clean your room, make your bed, offer twenty-four-hour room service and provide various forms of entertainment, including movie theatres, casinos, bingo, onboard shopping, shore excursions, and nightly stage lounge acts with comedians, singers, and Las Vegas-style music-dance extravaganzas.

Cruise lines offer travel packages as short as three-day "Island Weekenders" to around-the-world junkets that last up to three months. Popular destinations include Alaska, Mexico, the Caribbean, the Mediterranean, the Baltic Sea, the Hawaiian Islands, and the Orient. There are also theme cruises in which the music, movies, lounge entertainment, and conversation center around a particular theme such as country music, jazz, golf, or health and fitness.

149

Cruise lines also distinguish themselves by catering to particular age and income groups. There are cruises aimed at singles (casual dining attire, current, popular music, and late-night partying), families (supervised activities for children), retirees (more formal dining attire, non-physical activities like bingo, casinos, workshops, movies), and pampered ultra-rich (formal dining attire, attentive white-glove service). Make sure that your travel agent is aware of your age, income, and activity preferences before booking a cruise. Selecting a discount cruise through the Internet may save you money, but it may not obtain the particular atmosphere you are seeking. Generally, the longer the cruise, the older the passengers. Cruises taken during the summer months of July and August as well as during Christmas and school vacations tend to have more young children and teenage passengers than in other months.

RECOMMENDED RETIREE CRUISE LINES

Holland-America

Targeting mostly retirees. Clients age ranges are fifty-plus. Entertainment includes bingo, gambling, movie theatre, musical stage presentations each night, reading library, escorted shore excursions, spa, gym, swimming, extra care for disabilities, both formal and informal attire at dinners. Separate casual dining area.

Princess Grand Class Cruising

More luxurious travelling for retirees ranging in ages from fifty to seventy-five. Choices in dining rooms and entertainment. Comfortable, long cruises. Half of all rooms have balconies. Gym, spa, reading library, gambling, swimming, live entertainment. Escorted shore excursions. More expensive, but roomier.

Walt Disney Cruises Lines

For taking pre-teen grandchildren on holidays. Supervised activities for children leave grandparents free to enjoy themselves. Can combine cruise with Walt Disney Hotel Resort and Theme Park reservations for a discount. Moderate to expensive. Two out of seven dinners require formal attire.

Project Eight—Take the Grandkids on Vacation

If you have lovable grandchildren, and their parents are both working, you might consider playing the role of the "fairy godmother" and take the toddlers on a memorable vacation. It's a great way to reward good behavior, to influence impressionable minds, and be remembered fondly long after you are gone. There are a number of attractions and organizations that are geared to pleasing children, including Disney Theme Parks, Mid-Florida Theme Parks, and educational excursions with Elderhostel or Familyhostel.

Walt Disney has expanded its attractions in Florida. There are currently four huge independently located Disney Theme Parks, including the traditional Magic Kingdom, a plant and animal preserve called Animal Kingdom, a movie theme park called MGM Studios, and a world culture park called Epcot. Each of these entertainment parks takes a minimum of a day to navigate. They also have fifteen different independently located Disney World Resorts for vacationers with their own interconnecting Disney Bus Lines to take you to a theme park each day. These sprawling hotel complexes have their own specific themes, swimming pools, multiple restaurants, and accommodations to suit varying budgets and family sizes. Some examples of these resorts include The Wilderness Lodge, Disney's Board Walk, the Old Key West Resort, Disney's Dixie Landing, the Grand Floridian Resort and Spa, and a teaching resort called the Disney Institute where the grandparents can go golfing or take cooking, photography, or fitness classes while the children learn animation, television production, or drama classes.

Walt Disney also operates the Disney Cruise Line with a fleet of two floating resort ships—*Disney Magic* and *Disney Wonder*. They offer three to seven-day round-trip cruises out of Port Canaveral, Florida. They also offer family excursions, movie theme cruises, and honeymoon cruises. The great attraction of the Disney Cruise ships is that the staff is dedicated to entertaining the children during the day while grandma and grandpa relax and enjoy their own adult entertainment areas of the ship. You can also get combination vacation packages that include three days at sea, accommodations at a Disney World Resort on land, and four-day passes to the Disney Theme Parks.

If you tire of the Walt Disney vacations, there are about one hundred different major tourist attractions along the east-west route from Daytona to Tampa, Florida. Most of them make excellent one-day excursions for families with a car. Examples include a movie theme park called Universal Studios; the newly renovated Kennedy Space Center entertainment complex ; Sea World, with its display of whales, sea lions, sharks, manatees and penguins; Discovery Cove, a thirty-acre park where tourists wade or swim in shallow water with dolphins, gentle sting rays and tropical fish; Arabian Nights, an equestrian ninety-minute dinner show with Arabian horses and a fabled princess in distress; and Busch Gardens, a zoological theme park with 2,700 animals, various rides, and musical entertainment. Use the Internet or the phone to obtain specific brochures and discover what rides and attractions are suitable for your grandchildren's age group.

Elderhostel is an organization dedicated to providing relatively inexpensive educational vacations for retirees.

They offer accommodations and short courses on a variety of topics in many exotic locations in the United States, Canada, and Europe. They also have special week-long vacation learning packages called Inter-Generational Vacations for retirees who accompany their grandchildren during a ten-week period in July and August. These varied vacations may include an introduction to water-colors, dance, theatre, puppets, UFO museums, horseback riding, nature walks,bicycling, the history of Gettysburg, exploring plants and animals, visits to the Houston Space Center, outdoor camping and fishing, archeology, and Indian culture. All of them are unique educational experiences.

Familyhostel is a learning vacation program operated by the University of New Hampshire, Department of Continuing Education. They offer ten-day, escorted summer learning and travel programs to foreign countries in small groups of five to ten families who have school-age children from ages eight to fifteen. They offer sightseeing, hands-on experiences, and presentations on wildlife, culture, and arts and crafts of the host country being visited. Aunts, uncles, and grandparents, as well as parents, can substitute as the responsible accompanying adults. For more information on the excursions mentioned above, please refer to the following resources.

Website keywords:
Orlando Attractions
Orlando Vacation Planner
Disney World

Cruise Website:
www.disneycruisesvacationguide.com

Elderhostel Inc., U.S.A.
11 Avenue de Lafayette
Boston, MA 02111-1746
Website: www.elderhostel.org

This organization offers travel/learning vacations in every state of the union. In the U.S.A./Canada catalog, look in the section called Inter-Generational Tours.

Familyhostel
University of New Hampshire
Department of Continuing Education
6 Garrison Avenue
Durham, New Hampshire 03824
E-mail learn.dce@unh.edu
Website keyword: familyhostel

For vacations with young grandchildren ages eight to fifteen. This organization arranges overseas cultural immersion learning vacations. Small group with university tour guide.

Creative Retirement

Project Nine—Join a Seniors' Activity Center

Seniors' activity centers, sometimes called centers for seniors or senior community centers, are nonprofit, often city-sponsored organizations staffed largely by volunteers for the benefit of people in the area who are retired. A seniors' activity center supplies participants with two important retirement needs—a place to meet active people your own age and a variety of interesting things to do. It will appeal to several types of individuals simultaneously, including the socializer, organizer, volunteer, athlete, and intellectual.

These organizations vary somewhat from one location to another. To get an idea of what your local center is offering new members, ask for an escorted tour of the building while it's in operation, look at their activity bulletin board, and obtain a copy of their monthly newsletter. Their newsletter, more than anything else, quickly identifies the most common type and range of activities that the organization provides. A newsletter typically lists upcoming day and evening activities provided by the organization, such as workshops, seminars, banquets, theme celebrations (Halloween, St. Patrick's Day, Valentine's Day), group trips, and exercise classes. The best senior's groups have a balance of social, intellectual, and athletic activities for its members.

The social component of the seniors' center may include bridge and dart tournaments; lunches, and special banquets; day trips to art galleries, parks, and gambling casinos; and group holiday excursions in which a travel agent has arranged an escorted bus tour or cruise to some exotic location. For those who enjoy volunteering, the organization has need of ticket sellers, potluck cooks, table and chair assemblers, craft table organizers, special event decorators, workshop instructors, seminar leaders, and newsletter publicists.

The organization may consider education an important component of their program and offer workshops on how to play bridge, use computers, or master a range of interesting craft hobbies. They may also have guest speakers on occasion, to speak on a range of topics of interest to its members, such as health, traveling, art appreciation, and floral gardening.

Their athletic component may include stretching and light exercise classes, T'ai Chi, aqua-fitness, table tennis, and darts. Often, seniors' centers will negotiate low senior admissions and special senior classes at nearby swimming pools, tennis courts, and gyms for their members. Some organizations offer outside groups the use of their facilities in return for reduced admission to their activities for their members. Seniors' activity centers offer a range of things for retirees to do, see, make, and enjoy. Members can be observers, participants, or organizers of the events. In essence, there is something for everyone.

Project Ten—Do Something Entirely Different

With the loss of colleagues from work, grown children who have left home, and, on occasion, personal friends who have passed away, retirement typically involves an absence of comfortable social groups that provided companionship, celebration, and social interaction. There is a need for many retirees to reinvent and to explore new social circles.

In the British comedy series *Monty Python's Flying Circus,* the phrase "And Now for Something Completely Different" was frequently used as a transition to separate different humorous skits. It is also a useful phrase that many creative retirees have adopted in their approach to seeking new friends and social patterns. It suggests a creative, innovative, "out-of-the-box" style of thinking by seeking social activities and hobbies that one would not normally associate with traditional retirement. Here are five possibilities.

1. You might consider registering for a Star Trek Convention. These popular science fiction conferences are attended by people of all age groups and backgrounds. Many come dressed as Klingons, Star Trek officers, or Borgs and have even learned intergalactic songs and languages (Klingon Dictionaries are available for the uninitiated). Special guest stars from one of the three *Star Trek* series or from offshoots of the original series, such as *Deep Space Nine*, or *Andromeda*, are often guests at these conventions. These interesting speakers, along with colorful costumed characters in the audience, are sure to please. It's an entertaining place to meet

people who think creatively. If friends ask you where you are going, you can reply, "To seek out new life; to boldly go where no man/woman has gone before!"

2. If you enjoy singing, join a local choral group that meets weekly to practice singing popular songs, Gershwin tunes, barbershop quartet harmonies, or show tunes. They often give performances at concerts, sing Christmas carols in shopping malls, and provide entertainment at fall fairs. It's fun, sociable, and entertaining. Check the weekend entertainment section of your newspaper or your local television community channel for singing groups in your area.

3. People who enjoy researching family history might find genealogy conventions a fun place to meet people, learn new facts, and research techniques related to the popular hobby. Regional genealogy societies, in addition to national organizations, offer weekend series of workshops along with vendor displays of how-to books, maps, cemetery transcription booklets, and friendly people who love to share their knowledge of their favorite pastime. It's not uncommon for several hundred of these gatherings to take place between April and June of each year. Use the Internet to search for ones that are closest to you or in the area that you are researching.

4. One enduring hobby course that has a mix of men and women of varying ages is introductory photography. A group of fifteen to twenty people get together once a week in the evenings at local high schools, community colleges, during day classes in Elderhostel getaway excursions, or at the Disney Institute in Florida to learn

camera techniques, such as composition, lighting, and camera settings in an easy, friendly learning environment.

5. Active retirees might consider attending senior community center dances. You are guaranteed to find people in your own age bracket, although typically the women will outnumber the men. It's a great social setting for meeting people, getting a bit of exercise on the dance floor, and making new friends. Check the senior center monthly newsletter for upcoming events. For additional information, please refer to the following sources.

Science Fiction Conventions
Website: www.showcon.com
Website: www. conventions.fanspace.com

These are websites that list the locations and dates of upcoming sci-fi conventions in the United States and Canada. Some past locations: Los Angles, Las Vegas, Minneapolis, Tampa, Toronto.

Federation of Genealogy Societies
Website: www.fgs.org

This is a national association linking regional American societies together. Look up Conferences and Other Federations.

Chapter Ten

Projects For the Intellectual

Intellectuals enjoy expanding their minds. They seek out activities that teach them new skills or ideas and enjoy problem-solving, brainstorming, researching, teaching, and creative thinking. This chapter presents ten mind-expansion projects to help you grow intellectually during your retirement. Check off the projects that you might be interested in.

Projects in This Chapter: ✔

1. Retire in a Campus Community ☐
2. Combine Learning with Travel ☐
3. Earn a Certificate or Diploma ☐
4. Write a Nonfiction Book ☐
5. Use the Internet as a Research Tool ☐
6. Read a Book a Week for Fifty Weeks ☐
7. Travel Back to the Battle of Gettysburg ☐
8. Experience Washington, D.C. ☐
9. Become a Certified Genealogist ☐
10. Become a Bridge Player ☐

Creative Retirement

Project One—Retire in a Campus Community

For retirees who enjoy the intellectual stimulation of taking courses, attending guest lectures, or earning degrees, an exciting alternative lifestyle is available. It involves moving into retirement communities built on or near university property. A concept first started by retiring professors, several campus retirement communities in the United States and Canada have built campus communities specifically designed for retirees. People are drawn not just by the learning potential but by a range of university activities, including concerts and plays, evening guest lectures on everything from communications to politics, as well as residence-based activities such as swimming, exercise classes, card tournaments, and chats by the fireplace in the common room.

This lifestyle attracts both singles and couples who long for something more stimulating than long, lonely apartment corridors or empty-nest households. The campus accommodations are varied. Some offer attractive bungalows nestled in woodlands with walking trails, while others offer low-rise apartment suites. All of them offer easy campus access and common-room privileges. Some are restricted to people in their sixties and seventies, while others have a cluster of people of all ages including young families. Many communities have a specific theme or focus. The following are some examples of such communities:

The Senior Academy, a unique learning and cultural center for seniors, has been recently constructed in a beautiful mountain setting near Tucson, Arizona. It is a residential academy village connected with the

University of Arizona. It is designed to bring together individuals (sixty-five years and older) at the top of their professions—scholars, scientists, writers, artists, and executives—in an educational community where they can continue to be productive well into their retirement years. In addition to office space and classrooms, residents can participate in courses, seminars, workshops, Elderhostel programs, concerts, theatre, and ballet.

EcoVillage in Ithaca, New York, connected with Cornell University, is a multigenerational cohousing project with a quarter of the population of sixty residents over the age of fifty. The homes are tall with small rooms and use a minimum amount of land. Residents walk or jog along the village walkways and swim in the pond in the summertime. The ethos, as you might have guessed, promotes being environmentally friendly and conservation of resources. Ithaca has been argumentatively described as the most "enlightened" town in America. It's a liberal town with a natural food co-op, and restaurants offer organically grown produce and vegetarian meals.

The Mountain Meadows Community near Ashland, Oregon, is typical of the new-style retirement communities built from scratch with single-story homes, condominiums, rental apartments, and assisted-living apartments. This complex has a four-acre park, clubhouse, panoramic dining, recreational facilities, and classrooms. The park hosts concerts and barbecues. The nearby town of Ashland is home of the Oregon Shakespeare Festival and the site of Southern Oregon University, which boasts the second largest Learning in Retirement chapter in the United States.

Village by the Arboretum is a gated retirement community named for the varied forested area threaded with hiking trails near Guelph University, in Guelph, Ontario. Its residents are nearly all over sixty. The community has wide streets lined with bright, attractive brick bungalows and townhouses, and access to a common 43,000-square-foot community center that offers a swimming pool and exercise room. Activities include use of the campus library, taking university classes, attending weekly guest lectures, and being a member of campus computer club or the community's walking club. The Village by the Arboretum offers a superactive lifestyle for older people with an appeal for those who want to continue learning.

If you are thinking of moving to a retirement haven, and enjoy taking courses or having access to the rich learning and cultural environments that universities tend to provide, you might consider a retirement community with close proximity to a center of learning.

The Arizona Senior Academy
The University of Arizona
Dr. Henry Koffler, President
M. D. Johnson Building, R. 312
1111 North Cherry Avenue
Tuscon, Arizona 85721
Phone: 1-520-621-9660
Fax: 1-520-626-7800

Retirement community and cultural center for retired professionals sixty-five years of age or older. Located in the mountains near Tuscon, Arizona.

EcoVillage at Ithaca
Website: wwwecovillage.ithaca.ny.us

The Mountain Meadows Community
Website: www.mtmeadows.com

Village by the Arboretum
Website: www.heritagehomes.com

Choose a College Town for Retirement
by Joseph M. Lublow
Globe Pequot, 1999
ISBN   0762703938

This book compares sixty-four college and/or university towns in twenty-nine states. Sites were selected for adult learning courses, quality medical care, and a vibrant cultural life. Choices are offered for people of varying incomes and budgets and for those seeking towns with particular climates.

Project Two—Combine Learning With Travel

Elderhostel is a nonprofit, tax-exempt corporation that packages unique one-week, two-week, or month-long travel-study programs for retirees in the United States, Canada, and Europe. Participants travel to an urban or rural location where they take classes during the day and use free time after classes to explore the tourist sites. Annually, over one quarter of a million retirees attend Elderhostel sites in forty-eight countries around the world. The programs are designed as a combination learning and vacation experience. The venues include university campuses, ranches, parks, RV campgrounds, and scenic country towns.

Typically, participants take one to three noncredit courses, which often are a mix of hands-on, experiential, and group instructional courses. Courses cover a broad spectrum of interests including art, crafts, computer training, French-language instruction, cooking, politics, local history, psychology, and the study of the works of particular authors or musicians. Many courses are devoted to the outdoors and may involve fly fishing, canoeing, biking on inner-city trails, or hiking along nature trails with a guide. One course is dedicated to learning about palaeontology and includes a day-long field trip to assist a professor at a dinosaur dig site. Special format courses include a cross-country train excursion combined with onboard classes, outdoor classes that use recreational vehicles, and inter-generational courses that permit retirees to take their grandchildren. A sample of international courses include bicycling in Europe, exploring Tibet and the border kingdoms of China, bird watching in Ecuador, walking in England's north country, and exploring

Australia's Great Barrier Reef along with Australia's east coast tropical jungle.

The living accommodations tend to be spartan, often in campus dormitories, and the dining is often plain institutional food. The advantage of these excursions is the people you meet, and the fun of learning new things combined with a vacation in a new locale. A weekly learning vacation package at a North America site is around $400—courses, food, and lodging included. A twenty-day European, South American, or Australian tour is more expensive and might cost an average of $3,500 for the flight, courses, food, and lodging. Enrollment is restricted to people fifty-five years of age or older with companions not younger than fifty.

Interhostel and Familyhostel are two alternate travel study programs developed by the University of New Hampshire in 1980 to promote cross-cultural awareness. Interhostel programs, for people over fifty, are developed in cooperation with colleges, universities, and similar overseas institutions in the foreign region where the program will be held. Its experts lead presentations, lectures, mini-classes, and field trips. Costs include admission to museums and sightseeing, for an inside look at the country's people, art, history, culture, and philosophy. Your escort is usually a University of New Hampshire staff member.

Over sixty programs a year are offered in twenty-five countries all over the world, such as England, Ireland, France, Netherlands, Germany, Switzerland, China, and New England. Cost includes round-trip airfare, all activities, meals, accommodations, and ground transportation. Groups are kept small—about thirty to forty people from throughout the United States. Most programs are two weeks in length, but some are longer. There are lectures in the morning and tours in the afternoon. The focus is to teach the culture and history of the host country. Prices can range from $2,000 to $3,500, depending on the destination.

Familyhostel is a program designed for families with school-age children from ages eight to fifteen. It offers unique ten-day summer learning and travel programs to foreign countries. It is run by the University of New Hampshire Continuing Education, the same operators as Interhostel. Programs include presentations, hands-on workshops, sightseeing, culture, recreation, native arts and crafts, nature and wildlife, and social activities. Costs include round-trip airfare, ground transportation all activities, meals, family-style accommodations near parks, woods, and playgrounds. Groups are kept small—five to ten families from throughout the United States. Children must be accompanied by a responsible adult, whether it be the parents, grandparents, or aunts and uncles.

TraveLearn is a leading tour company that specializes in educational tours and travel. It caters to adults from ages thirty to eighty and prides itself in providing topnotch university tour guides and luxury accommodation with hot showers, private bathrooms and great food. Typical overseas travel/learning packages run about $2,000 to $3,000 per person and offer travel groups ranging in size from fifteen to twenty people. For additional information, refer to the following resources.

Elderhostel Inc., U.S.
11 Avenue de Lafayette
Boston, Massachusetts
02111-1746
Tel: (617)-426-7788
Website: www.elderhostel.org

Minimum age requirement is fifty-five years old. Companion must be at least fifty years old. Each year, Elderhostel publishes four catalogs for venues in North America, four catalogs for international venues and four supplemental catalogs which includes programs for people with RVs and programs on water (cruises, paddlewheel excursions). Catalog subscription fee $10 US funds or $14 Canadian funds.

Routes to Learning Canada
4 Cataraqui Street
Unit 300
Kingston, Ontario
K7K 1Z7
Tel: (613)-530-2222
Fax: (613)-530-2096
Toll Free: 1-877-426-8056
E-mail: ecmail@elderhostel.org
Website: www.routestolearning.ca

This organization also manages Elderhostel Canada. They offer similar programs to Elderhostel U.S.but concentrate on travel-learning programs in Canada. Glossy catalogue of provincial tours available. No age limitations as with Elderhostel, but definitely geared to retirees.

Interhostel/Familyhostel
University of New Hampshire
Continuing Education
6 Garrison Avenue
Durham, New Hampshire 03824
E-mail: learn.dce@unh.edu
Website keyword: Interhostel

The University of New Hampshire hosts two educational tour groups, Interhostel (for adults) and Familyhostel (for adults with children).

TraveLearn
Website: www.travelearn.com

Early retirees will appreciate the lack of age restrictions in this tour group. The website offers photo galleries of past trips, newspaper articles, and comments from the participants.

Project Three—Earn a Certificate or Degree

You may now wish that you had gone to university and completed a diploma, or that you had pursued a diploma that you really wanted, while your parents, or economic conditions, or other circumstances dictated something else. You now have the time, the maturity, the insight, and the investments to really enjoy the pursuit of this goal. What is it that you would like to learn?

Most colleges and universities make special accommodations for adult admissions. They often waive the requirement for a high school diploma for mature adults, assuming that life experience has provided an effective substitute. Many post-high school institutions also offer the alternative for people to "audit" a course; that is, they are allowed to attend the classes, but not submit assignments, write the exams, or receive any course credits. Auditing a course is less expensive ($20 versus $250, for example) and is a great way to discover whether or not you will like college classes or if you prefer to learn a subject without the pressure of exams.

Write or phone your local community college or university and ask them to send you a course description calendar (booklet) and admission requirements for mature students. Specify which calendar you would prefer, based on your area of interest—arts and sciences, computer science, journalism, sociology, business, etc. You may also wish to inquire about a possible tour of the campus. Generally classes run summer and winter and include day and evening classes.

It is helpful to have a computer and printer for doing assignments if you choose to enrol and seek credits towards a degree. Also, you need casual clothing and a car, or you need to have access to a direct bus route to the campus. Courses generally cost $250-$500 each, plus the cost of books and classroom writing materials for taking notes.

Virtual Universities

A more recent option that you may wish to explore is called the virtual university, university courses offered over the Internet. Your lessons, exams, and assignments appear on your computer screen at home and you submit your assignments by mail, e-mail, or fax. Often, you will be required to purchase course textbooks through the university bookstore or Amazon.com.

This method has several advantages, which include learning at your own pace and at the time of your choosing, not having to commute to classes, and having access to a virtual community of university course offerings from anywhere in the world. For example, you may wish to take a course in journalism from one university and a course in marine biology from another. You pay for your courses over the Internet, or by phone, with a credit card. The main disadvantages of the virtual university are that not all courses are offered this way, and you may never get to see or discuss course content with your instructor or tutor except through e-mail. This makes the courses slightly more difficult compared with traditional methods of delivery. Independent and self-directed individuals, however, may find this method quite comfortable.

VIRTUAL UNIVERSITY WEBSITES

World Lecture Hall
Website: www.utexas.edu/world/lecture

This University of Texas at Austin website provides links to university courses offered worldwide in any language.

Worldwide Web Virtual Library
Website: www.cisnet.com

This website offers links to a number of virtual education sites in Australia, United Kingdom, France, Canada, and the United States.

Project Four—Write a Nonfiction Book

Write a nonfiction, self-help, or reference book on some topic that you enjoy and feel passionate about. This project may require in-depth research in libraries, on the Internet, or through personal interviews with people. It may require organizing of material into a logical sequence, creating interesting text, and using a computer system. It will require an analysis of your target market and who is to be the typical reader.

This is a project that can be both creative and financially rewarding. People of all ages seek books in the self-help section of the bookstore when they need expertise in some area. After living fifty or sixty years, you have accumulated a lot of knowledge and expertise in some field. Write a book about one aspect of it, and share that knowledge with other people.

The list of topics in which people are interested appear endless. Visit a bookstore and look at the kind of nonfiction and self-help books that people are buying. Titles include cooking, flower gardening, Japanese gardening, dating, retirement, investing, photography, repairing automobiles, sailing, knitting, sewing your own clothes, stamp collecting, coin collecting, exercising, and healing emotional hurt.

The chances of getting published will increase if the manuscript approaches an old topic in a new way or if the book is about something interesting, but few authors have written about it. The more the manuscript differs from similar titles currently on store bookshelves, the more an editor will like it. Editors are looking for new, fresh material. Large publishing houses will not accept unsolicited manuscripts. They prefer that a literary agent prescreen your material before presenting it to them. Literary agents offer their services in return for 15 to 20 percent of the net royalties paid to the author. Smaller regional book companies, however, may accept unsolicited materials if the topic fits their publishing interests. Always submit a short query letter first explaining the proposal and include a sample double-spaced chapter along with a self-addressed stamped envelope for their reply. For more information on writing and publishing, you may wish to consult these references.

Is There a Book Inside You?
by Dan Poynter, Mindy Bingham
Para Publishing, 1998, 5th Edition,
ISBN 1568600461

This popular reference will help you to pick a topic, break it down into easy steps, pinpoint where to do research and to evaluate your publishing options.

Writing Successful Self-Help & How-To Books
by Jean Marie Stine
John Wiley & Sons, Ltd., 1997
ISBN 0471037397

The author has edited over 50 self-help books. Topics include choosing the right title, book proposals, and the importance of interactive features, such as checklists, quizzes, and exercises.

Damn! Why Didn't I Write That?
By Marc McCutcheon
Quill Driver Press, 2001
ISBN 1884956173

An excellent reference for beginning nonfiction writers. Topics include nonfiction success stories, choosing a saleable topic, query letters, book proposals, negotiating contracts, promotion, and writing techniques. Highly motivating and easy to read.

Project Five—Use the Internet as a Research Tool

Surveys of Internet use have indicated that the largest cluster of Internet users after teenagers are retirees. People use the Internet for a variety of reasons, including socializing (chat rooms, e-mailing pen pals), organizing (hotel, car, cruise, and concert reservations), commercial transactions (purchase of products and services), data retrieval, and research. It is the latter function that may provide the greatest use to those who are intellectually minded.

The Internet can provide an array of support services for academics, writers, and professionals, such as semi-retired doctors, engineers, and lawyers who wish to keep up to date in their field, retirees pursuing additional courses or degrees, and ordinary people who are just curious about something.

The Internet provides both free and fee-related technical information on just about any subject you can think of. Internet search engines are capable of scanning databases worldwide and can bring you relevant information from several continents, not just from your own country. There are three things that you might concentrate on that will make your searches more productive: the best research search engines, effective search techniques, and websites with your favorite information.

The best search engines for research are metasearch engines, such as Google.com, Mamma.com, or Metacrawler.com, that seek out the assistance of other browsers to find information for you. They are useful for seeing the quantity of information available on the web on a particular topic. Other helpful search engines include "natural language" systems that permit the user to submit questions, and "menu" search engines that present the user with a menu of options organized by category. Choose menu search engines that are geared to looking up concepts, ideas, and references, as opposed to those which cater to the general public and consumer purchases. Try these three search engines, each with a different style of operation.

Google
www.google.com

A metasearch engine that checks dozens of other search engines simultaneously. Great way to find out how much information about your topic is out there on the Internet.

Ask Jeeves!
www.askjeeves.com

A "natural language" search engine that permits the user to ask questions like "Who invented the laser?"

Yahoo
www.yahoo.com

The oldest and best menu-style search engine for launching research queries. Twelve out of fourteen categories are pure research-oriented items. Reference Category has an additional 29 sub-categories.

RESEARCH TECHNIQUES

Effective search techniques incorporate the use of mathematical + and - signs, quotation marks around a phrase, and boolean operators (for example, AND NOT OR) to narrow and focus your search. The words "Advanced Search" near the top of most major search engine main menus will teach you the techniques.

Your favorite research websites should be bookmarked so that you can return to them quickly and directly when they are required.

ADDITIONAL RESEARCH WEBSITES

Information Please Almanac
www.infopls.com
Like having a stack of reference books inside your computer.

iTools
www.itools.com
An assortment of research tools including 13 research features: a language identifier, language translator, law definitions, and a rhyming dictionary to name a few.

Internet Public Library
www.ipl.org
This website is operated by the University of Michigan and includes a graphic main menu that looks like a library.

Starting Page
www.startingpage.com/index

This website lists several categories to assist the researcher, including several metasearch engines.

Project Six—Read a Book a Week For Fifty Weeks

A frequent complaint from people during their work-ing and childbearing years is that there never seems to be enough time for intellectual pursuits and for the reading of good books in particular. Retirement provides the solution with both a quiet, nonhectic environment and plenty of unscheduled time. Whether you live in a house in the suburbs or a high-rise apartment building in a bustling city, there are certain times in the day that provide a perfect setting for concentrated reading.

One laudable goal that you might consider setting for yourself is to read one book a week for fifty weeks, so that by the end of a year you have read fifty books at a reasonable pace, with two weeks off for holidays. A second goal that you might set for yourself is not to select books at random, but rather to target specific authors, genres, subjects, or categories, so as to maximize the intellectual benefits of your effort.

For example, there are book clubs and women's discussion groups across the country that meet once a month to share what they have learned from their fiction reading. Generally, they read and discuss themes and writing styles, as well as plots, with the other members of their group.

Another approach to fiction reading is to select a cer-tain author who is considered to be popular and suc-cessful and read their entire collection of novels. You will become both knowledgeable of their work and develop a strong insight into their writing styles. For past authors, consider borrowing the books from the public library. They have already organized entire collections by multiple authors, and you do not have to purchase the books.

A third approach to reading fiction is to choose a favorite genre—mystery, romance, western, horror, fantasy, science fiction, or drama—and concentrate on books from that genre.

The nonfiction reader might consider choosing books by subject or category rather than by author. The goal of nonfiction readers to is improve their understanding and expertise in a certain area. It may be politics, biographies, investing, website programming, gardening, cooking, physical fitness, psychology, sociology, health, self-improvement, and so on. The idea is to concentrate your reading on a specific topic, or clusters of several topics, during the year. The library may also provide an inexpensive source of reading, and they already have the nonfiction items organized by topic.

Only you can decide what types of books appeal to you the most during the fifty weeks. If you are unsure where to start, take a trip to the public library and peruse the shelves to see what interests you. Is it fiction or nonfiction? What authors and topics appear intriguing? Once you have decided, begin week one. For additional resources, refer to the following list.

The Book Group Book
by Ellen Slezak and Margaret Atwood,
Chicago Review Printers. 2000, 2nd Edition
ISBN 1556524129

This thoughtful guide to forming and enjoying a stimulating book discussion group is organized into 46 essays that describe how individual groups are organized, and how to select members, and stimulate discussions. Highly recommended.

How to Read a Book
by Adler and Van Doren
Simon & Schuster, 1972
ISBN   0671212095

This classic book, first published in 1940, is still in print. The book breaks down the levels of reading: Elementary, Inspectional, Analytical, and Synoptical. Helpful to nonfiction readers wanting to get more understanding out of what they read.

Project Seven—Travel Back to the Battle of Gettysburg

Cast-iron cannons and solemn bronze monuments lining the roadside signal to visitors that they have arrived in historic Gettysburg, Pennsylvania, site of perhaps the most famous battle of the American Civil War. Here, for three hot days in July of 1863, Union and Confederate soldiers faced off in a bloody conflict that left some fifty-one thousand casualties. The resulting Confederate defeat is regarded by many historians as the turning point in the war. Consecrating a national military cemetery near the site the following November, President Abraham Lincoln delivered a two-minute speech—The Gettysburg Address—considered one of the most eloquent in modern history.

The town of Gettysburg has more than one hundred nineteenth-century buildings restored to their original Civil War charm. The tourist district has three museums including the Soldiers' National Museum, the Hall of Presidents and First Ladies, and the National Civil War Museum, as well as the Old Gettysburg Village, a re-creation of the former pioneer town.

The nearby five-thousand-acre Military Park with its ridges and ravines has forty miles of roads and paths winding around the landmarks of the battle. There are more than one thousand markers and monuments to commemorate the key events of the battle. The Visitor Center rents or sells audiocassette tours that re-create the historic three-day battle complete with commentary and sound effects as you drive through the battlefield at your own pace. There are also two-hour narrated double-decker bus tours and a five-hour narrated tour on the Gettysburg Railroad Steam Train. The National Cemetery, adjacent to the battlefield, is a lovely well-shaded spot for a summer stroll or a genealogy field trip.

In addition to visiting General Lee's headquarters and Lincoln Square, the retirement home of a president from a different era, Dwight D. Eisenhower, is also in the same area and open for viewing. Visitors staying overnight may wish to sleep in the Best Western Gettysburg Hotel, which was built and decorated to resemble the architecture and furnishings of the Civil War era. Gettysburg is an exciting audiovisual adventure into an important part of America's history and is well worth an extended vacation. Additional information may be obtained through the following sources.

Gettysburg Official Website
Website: www.gettysburg.com

Contains information on motels and hotels, bed and breakfasts, campgrounds, tours, attractions, and weather forecasts for the area. Also portal to Visitors Information Center to help plan your trip.

Gettysburg Tour Center
778 Baltimore Street
Gettysburg, Pennsylvania 17325
Phone: 717-334-6296

The location to obtain tickets for bus and train excursions or walkabout tours, maps, audiotapes of the battle.

The Battle of Gettysburg: A Guided Tour
by Stackpole, Gottfried, and Nye
Stackpole Books, 1998
ISBN   0811726762

The official paperback tour book used for the past 30 years, updated with photos and maps. Price: $6.25

Gettysburg (movie)
Available: Amazon.com

Excellent 1993 movie of the epic Civil War battle of Gettysburg that depicts the clash from both the Northern and Southern viewpoints. Entertaining and easy-to-follow storyline. Available on VHS or DVD formats. Huge cast stars Martin Sheen and Tom Berenger. Great pre or post-tour overview.

Project Eight—Experience Washington D.C.

The ten square miles of Washington, D.C. is a symbol of America. This beautiful two hundred-year-old metropolis on the banks of the Potomac River is the envy of the world. It's not only the seat of the nation's government, with the White House, Congress, Senate and Pentagon. The impressive neighboring institutions, wide streets, parks, monuments, museums, and archives speak of the greatness, power, pride, and history of its people. It belongs to all of its nation's citizens, and it's a moving experience for the eighteen million or more sightseers who visit there each year.

Retirees who enjoy politics and history could easily spend a week in the capital city exploring the Smithsonian Institution with its fourteen museums, taking a free self-escorted White House tour (open Tuesdays-Saturdays 10 A.M.—noon), and visiting the Jefferson Memorial, the peaceful and contemplative Lincoln Memorial (considered by some to be the most moving monument), and the Washington Monument, a 555 foot-tall obelisk that punctuates the city like a huge exclamation point. People can say that they have "done" Washington if they have strolled from the Capitol to the Lincoln Memorial and visited all the museums and monuments in between.

Visitors new to the city might consider taking an escorted tour to get an overview of the various attractions. Tour Mobiles offer several narrated tours, including one that stops at eighteen historic sites and museums between the Capitol and the Arlington Cemetery. When on foot, the Mall, where nine of the

Smithsonian museums and numerous other attractions are gathered, is the place most visitors head for first.

There are two war-related sites that are worth seeing for their historical significance. The first is the United States Holocaust Memorial Museum. It dramatizes the tragedy, horror, and heroism of the Nazi years. The emotional displays unfold chronologically from 1933-1945, from the Nazi rise to power to the liberation and its aftermath. The second site is the outdoor Vietnam Veterans' Memorial, a black V-shaped granite monument inscribed with the names of more than forty-eight thousand Americans who died in the war. The various tributes, such as medals, Army boots, cards, and trinkets, left at the Veterans' Memorial are collected each evening by the attendants and submitted to a Vietnam War Archive for preservation.

One additional attraction worth seeing is the 163-acre National Zoological Park where four thousand animals from more than five hundred species are displayed, including cheetahs capable of sixty-mile-an-hour bursts of speed in the wild and the cuddly-looking giant panda bears who rely entirely on bamboo branches, stems, and leaves for sustenance. For evening entertainment, check the local newspaper or the Washington website for seasonal concerts, stage plays, and special events. For additional information, please refer to the following sources.

The Official Washington Website
www.washington.org
Also keyword: Washington DC

This official comprehensive website can be used to plan a vacation to the capital city. It lists hotels, motels, restaurants, attractions, maps, and brochures. Information is available in English, Spanish, French, and German.

Washington Visitors Information Center
1455 Pennsylvania Avenue, N.W.
Washington, D.C.
Telephone: 202-328-4748
Website: www.dcvisit.com

On-site drop-in center. Useful for getting directions, suggestions, and brochures. Also available on the Internet.

White House Visitors Center
Website: www.whitehouse.gov/tours/
Information Line: 202-456-7041

This is the place where public tour tickets for White House Tours are obtained. The Visitors Center can take up to 1½ hours to go through, while the White House self-guided tour takes about 20 minutes. There are no rest rooms on the tour and cameras are not permitted. (Note: Escorted White House tours can be arranged through your local Congressman.)

Creative Retirement

Project Nine—Become a Certified Genealogist

One hobby that ranks high in popularity among this current generation of retirees is genealogy, or the researching of one's family history. Specifically, genealogy refers to the study, tracing, and recording of family pedigrees—the descent of a person or family from a set of ancestors. There are a number of magazines, workshops, and conferences that focus on this specific pastime. There are so many people interested in their family trees, in fact, that many individuals hire researchers by the hour to help them "dig up" their ancestors.

This fascination with family trees and the request for certified researchers has prompted hobbyists to seek the designation of "professional genealogist." This is a person who adheres to and promotes high-quality standards and scholarship in research. There are two leading credentialing systems in the United States: accreditation by the Church of Latter Day Saints and certification by the Board of Certification of Genealogists.

The Family History Library of the Church of Jesus Christ of the Latter Day Saints began its accreditation program in 1964. To become accredited, you must complete an application and take a supervised exam. Parts of the exam include document recognition, document transcription, case studies, concentration in a regional area, and an interview through which you explain and verbally defend what you have done. You will also need to complete a research project.

The Board of Certification of Genealogists in Washington, D.C. was initiated several years ago by a group of professional genealogists. The Board grants certification in three research categories: Certified Genealogist (CG), emphasizing compiling genealogies in all lines of descent; Certified Genealogist Record Specialist (CGRS), which emphasizes use of genealogy records; and the newly defined Certified Lineage Specialist (CLS), which emphasizes researching and compiling multigenerational lineages. The Board also offers secondary certification in two teaching categories: Certified Genealogical Instructor (CGI) and Certified Genealogical Lecturer (CGL).

Accreditation is more popular in the western United States because of its closeness to Salt Lake City and the Church of the Latter Day Saints. Certification is more popular in eastern United States. Legally, you do not need either designation to offer your services as a genealogist. However, it adds to your credibility as a business person.

There is a third institution that both teaches courses in genealogy and certifies its graduates. The National Institute for Genealogical Studies at the University of Toronto offers a series of twenty-four courses grouped into three levels (Basic, Intermediate, and Advanced) that leads to a Certificate in Genealogical Studies. Offered by the Department of Continuing Education at University of Toronto, it is the first such certificate in North America that is provided entirely over the Internet. Current registrants include people from California, Texas, Louisiana, Alaska, and Canada.

Individuals may sign up for the full certificate program or take one course at a time to suit their needs. Family historians, librarians, archivists, and those seeking to provide professional genealogical services to users are among the registrants. Each Monday morning, an e-mail introduces the topic for the week. Students retrieve the lessons and submit their completed assignments by e-mail or to a Web Board Discussion Group with an instructor. The weekly assignments will take five to eight hours to complete. Each course take six weeks to complete. An online exam will conclude each course.

Topics include Research Methodology, Using the Family History Centers of the Latter Day Saints, Internet Resources, Census Records, Vital Statistics, Wills and Estate Records, and Land Records. The assignments increase in complexity with each of the three levels of the certificate program. You can also specialize in American, English, Scottish, Canadian, or French-Canadian programs. Each course costs $50. Those who register for all eight courses of level one will be charged a discounted fee of $325. It's a great way to expand your knowledge of an interesting hobby from the comfort and privacy of your own home. For additional information, refer to the following sources.

Board for Certification of Genealogists
P. O. Box 14291
Washington, D.C. 84150
Website: www.bcgcertification.org

This organization has a helpful website with an area to test your current skills, a recommended standards manual, and instructions on how to apply for certification.

Accreditation Committee
35 North West Temple Street
Salt Lake City, Utah 84150

This is the committee in charge of the Family History Library, accepting applications, administering exams, and granting accreditation for the Church of the Latter Day Saints.

National Institute for Genealogical Studies
30 Wellington Street East
Suite 2002
Toronto, Ontario
Canada M5E 1S3
Phone: 416-861-0165
E-mail: info@genealogicalstudies.com
Website: www.genealogicalstudies.com

You can obtain a descriptive brochure through the website or by writing their office. The brochure outlines the three levels of difficulty and course requirements leading to certification.

Family Chronicle
Moorshead Magazines Ltd.
505 Consumers Road Suite 500
Toronto, M2J 4V8 Canada
Website: www.familychronicle.com

One of the better magazines for genealogy hobbyists in North America. Covers broad range of topics including American Civil War, American immigration patterns, various ethnic colonialist groups. Helpful advertisements, book and software reviews.

RETIREMENT TIP

While small towns are fun to explore on a whim, excursions to major cities work best when the little details are worked out ahead of time, such as hotel reservations, directions, and brochures of sights to see.

Project Ten—Become a Bridge Player

Writer W. Somerset Maugham once said, "Bridge is the most entertaining and intellectual card game of wit man has so far devised." He may be right because this partnership game is loved and played by millions of people worldwide. Most communities, both large and small, have a bridge club with weekly meetings and annual team competitions. In addition to bridge clubs, bridge hands often appear printed in the entertainment section of the newspaper, games are played between partners on the Internet, and companies have devised elaborate bridge software games for computer users.

Bridge involves skill, chance, personal strategy, communication with a partner, and uniqueness of the deal. There are no fewer than 53,644,737,765, 488,792,839,237,440,000 possible deals in any one game, so you are unlikely to ever see the same game occur twice in your lifetime, even if you play every day. Because every hand is different, the intellectual challenge of bridge never ceases. Certain principles, however, are useful in many different situations, and their mastery is rewarding to the students of the game.

The basic elements of playing bridge involve four players, thirteen cards each, bidding (stating to the group what suit will be trump and a promise to take more tricks than all the opponents), playing cards by following suit with the leader, and winning a trick if your high card beats all the others. There are a total of thirteen tricks per deal.

The basic mechanics of the game can be learned fairly quickly, although learning to bid, using strategy to outmaneuvre your opponents, and communicating effectively with your partner are skills that take time and practice. Husband and wife teams should learn the game together to ensure that the skill levels increase simultaneously to avoid frustrating your partner. Software games of bridge with varying degrees of difficulty may also prove helpful in learning the game.

Retirees are great bridge players and can be found playing at house card parties, in apartment buildings, at local seniors' bridge clubs, and on long ocean cruises. The game can be quite addictive, however, as the following true story indicates. One day in a New York bridge club, a foursome were enjoying their regular noon-hour game when one of the four, an attractive young woman, looked at her watch and announced to the surprise of those at the table, "I'm sorry to have to break up this very pleasant game, but I'm getting married in half an hour," and promptly left. The other three were visibly disappointed, but were somewhat understanding and instinctively looked around the room for a replacement card player.

For additional information on this hobby, refer to the following sources.

The Complete Idiot's Guide to Bridge
by Anthony Medley, and Alan Lebebdig
Macmillan, 1997
ISBN 0028617355

This book provides the information you need to understand how to play bridge. Includes basic play, scoring, bidding, and deducing information from the others' bids.

Bridge for Dummies
by Edwin Kantar, and Eddie Kantar
Hungry Minds, Inc., 1997
ISBN 0764550152

An introduction to the basics of bridge playing. Includes discussions on the finer points of tricks, bids contracts, and strategy. Explains the "why" behind the conventions.

Chapter Eleven

Projects For the Volunteer/Caregiver

A volunteer/caregiver is a person who enjoys helping
other people. He/she often obtains personal satisfaction
and self-esteem from focusing on other people.
Caregivers do not need encouragement to help others.
It usually comes naturally. This chapter will present
ten creative projects that allow you to behave in a caring
manner and combine other needs and desires at the
same time, such as traveling, organizing, and socializing.
Check off the projects that you might be interested in.

Projects in This Chapter: ✔

1. Volunteer Your Career Skills ☐
2. Support Your Local Hospital ☐
3. Be a Driver for "Meals On Wheels" ☐
4. Support a Charity Bazaar ☐
5. Visit a Shut-In ☐
6. Wrap Gifts for Charity ☐
7. Volunteer at the Seniors' Center ☐
8. Help the Humane Society ☐
9. Be a Food Bank Volunteer ☐
10. Run for Charity ☐

Project One—Volunteer Your Career Skills

Many skilled professionals view retirement as a time to change the way they work rather than a time to stop working completely. The knowledge and skills that professionals, such as doctors, nurses, and engineers, and tradespeople, such as carpenters and masons, accumulate after thirty years of service is substantial. But more importantly, their skills are portable, desirable, and much in demand, both domestically and globally.

One way for successful and active professionals to ease their transition into retirement is to volunteer their career skills through an agency that specializes in helping people in less developed countries, or in less wealthy neighborhoods of our own country. The change in location and the different pace will be like a vacation from the stressful demands of your usual lifestyle. A six-month or one-year assignment helping others while doing what you love may be a gift for your soul and a crowning achievement to your career. Recipients will be grateful, and your efforts can make a big difference in people's lives.

If the assignment is out of the country, the organizing agency may, particularly if you are a doctor, nurse, engineer, or project manager, book your flight, find a residence for you to live in, and provide you with insurance and living expenses while you live in that country. You also get an opportunity to explore their language, customs, and culture during your stay. However, be forewarned: working conditions will often be primitive and the work hard and challenging.

The assignment may also be in your own country, such as in a small town or village, or in a remote location in a sparsely populated area, or in a disaster-striken area, where your skills are needed. The agency will usually arrange for transportation and living accommodations.

Doctors Without Borders is the world's largest independent charitable emergency medical aid organization. It runs hospitals, sets up feeding stations for starving children, performs emergency surgery, and trains local health care personnel. It also manages massive vaccination campaigns in areas of the world where the health care system has broken down or is nonexistent, or in areas of immense poverty, and sometimes in the midst of war and violence, such as in Bosnia, Africa, or South America. Retired doctors, nurses, water and sanitation experts, logistics experts, and project managers can obtain postings through this agency.

Global Volunteers, a nonprofit organization based in St. Paul, Minnesota, coordinates more than 125 teams of volunteers who participate in prepackaged, short-term human development projects in twenty countries. Some volunteers teach business skills or English as a second language. Others build, repair, and paint community centers and classrooms; dig wells, build water systems; plant gardens; or help set up medical clinics. Teachers, engineers, nurses, and carpenters can get assignments through this organization.

Global Volunteers must arrange and pay for all their own expenses including travel, food, and lodging. The rewards are the encounters and camaraderie and friendship of the people that you are helping.

International locales include Eastern Europe, China, Mexico, Spain, Pakistan, Indonesia, and Vietnam. Local needy communities include Texas, Oklahoma, and South Carolina.

Carpenters and electricians can volunteer their skills in disaster-torn areas where entire neighborhoods have been demolished by hurricanes or tornados. Many missionary facilities are funded by multi-denominational religious groups. Disaster areas have both the Red Cross and government-funded agencies assisting with the rebuilding of schools and hospitals.

Habitat for Humanity International is a nonprofit, ecumenical Christian housing ministry that uses donations and volunteer labor in partnership with the target homeowner to build affordable housing for the poor. This is the agency that former President Jimmy Carter and President George W. Bush volunteered their time and carpentry skills to. Ongoing housing projects can be found in Georgia, Mississippi, Colorado, Kentucky, and Washington state. The Elderhostel programs organize week-long construction jaunts to these sites, including food and accommodation for approximately $400 starting in July. For further information on these organizations, you may wish to refer to the following sources.

Doctors Without Borders U.S.A.
6 East 39th Street, 8th floor
New York, NY 10016
Phone: 1-212-679-6800
Fax: 1-212-679-7016
E-mail   doctors@newyork.msf.org
Website: www.dwb.org/index

Creative Retirement

This organization seeks retired doctors, nurses, sanitation engineers, logistics experts, and project managers to work in medical emergency situations overseas.

Doctors Without Borders Canada
E-mail: msfcan@msf.ca
Website: www.msf.ca

Global Volunteers
375 E. Little Canada Road
St. Paul, Minneapolis
Phone: 1-800-487-1074
Fax: 1-651-482-0915
Website: http://www.globalvolunteers.org/

This nonprofit organization accepts retired teachers, engineers, nurses, and carpenters who assist in worldwide poverty situations.

Habitat for Humanity International
c/o Elderhostel U.S.A.
75 Federal Street
Boston, Massachussetts 02110
1-877-426-8056

This nonprofit Christian housing ministry accepts retirees skilled in the trades of carpentry, plumbing, painting, and dry-walling. One-week jaunts can be arranged through Elderhostel US/Canada Look under the "Services" category in their catalog.

Project Two—Support Your Local Hospital or Hospice

Everyone knows a friend or relative who has benefited from the pain-reducing or life-saving capabilities of a local hospital. You may have personally experienced the patience and kindness of the hospital staff. Perhaps it's time to give something back. Public hospitals and clinics under tight budgets usually welcome volunteer retirees. A "volunteer station," an area where volunteers check in for their assignments, is often located close to the reception desk.

The director of volunteer services actively seeks out applicants with various career skills, such as sales, retailing, counseling, clerical, social work, and child care that fit easily into the existing volunteer roles within the hospital. For example, a former retailer may be offered a role in the gift shop selling cards, balloons, candy, and gifts to visitors. He/she may also look after a refreshment stand that sells coffee, juice, and candy to people visiting their loved ones. Others may deliver flowers and mail to hospital rooms, or offer patients hot chocolate and cookies as a bedtime snack. Retirees with clerical skills may serve as filing clerks to take the work load off the nursing staff or to serve as a front-desk receptionists greeting visitors and directing them to various parts of the building. Some hospitals will show volunteers a list of current positions that are open and ask if any of the roles look interesting.

Volunteers with strong "people skills" may wish to serve as greeters, seeking out lonely patients who have no friends or relatives to visit them. They sit and chat with patients to cheer them up. A thoughtful volunteer can help to calm patients with a fear of hospitals or of surgery or image scanners in particular. Former salespeople are particularly good at this role.

There are a number of volunteer roles that require a small amount of training under the supervision of the nursing staff. "Cradle Care," for example, looks after newborn babies whose mothers have returned home to look after other family members. The infants need to be held, rocked, fed, burped, and have their diapers changed. Volunteers can assist the pediatric staff with these tasks.

Another role that requires some initial training is taking care of ambulatory patients who need assistance to walk to the floor lounge with their attached monitors. They need a break from the drab curtains and four walls of the hospital room to brighten their day.

A empathetic religious person might consider helping the hospital chaplain. In addition to ministers, priests, and rabbis, volunteers can be trained by chaplains to serve as nondenominational chaplain assistants to pray with patients approaching death and help give them some peace of mind.

When applying as a volunteer, mention your role preferences and times when you are available. The director will attempt to accommodate your wishes and will appreciate your offer of kindness.

Another support agency, often associated with hospitals, is hospice. This is a unique group of professionals that offers physical, spiritual, emotional, and social support to patients who are terminally ill, and their families. The support takes the form of time-off for the primary caregiver, as well as personal care, nutritional, pastoral, and grief counseling, and help with legal and funeral arrangements. There are 2,500 hospices in the United States with over 90 percent of the care being provided in the patient's home. Trained volunteers can offer respite care for family members as well as meaningful support to the patient. Discuss volunteer opportunities with the director of your local agency.

Project Three—Be a Driver For "Meals On Wheels"

If you don't mind driving around a small section of your town or city during the day, you might consider giving some of your time to a helpful community outreach program called "Meals On Wheels." The people who operate this low-profile service vary by community and may include nursing associations, religious or nonreligious charities, or municipal services. With the help of volunteer drivers, such as yourself, they deliver hot meals and vitamin-enriched drinks to house-bound recipients who are unable to care adequately for themselves. Recipients include the elderly, hospital patients recovering at home after surgery, and people with minor paralysis, muscle or spinal pain, or debilitating arthritis. Generally, the clients live alone and have no relatives or friends to care for them, and because of their infirmity they find it difficult to prepare their own dinner.

Hot nutritious meals are prepared once a day by the agency and placed in sealed compartmentalized trays, resembling TV dinners. Stacks of these dinners, along with separate hot or cold drinks, are placed in deep thermal carry bags to hold their temperature, and the driver places them in his or her vehicle and heads off on a predetermined route to deliver them in person to grateful clients.

One gets a strong sense of satisfaction from this volunteer act because in most cases, you may be the only human contact that these people will have during the day. Your smile and friendly manner become as important to them as the food you bring. They feel that at least one person in the world cares for them on that particular day.

To find out how to become one of their drivers, look up "Meals On Wheels" in the white pages of your telephone book. When you call the manager, explain that you are a retired person, and that you are thinking of volunteering your services as a driver, but would like to learn a bit more about the agency. Ask if you can visit their office and perhaps go out on a route with one of their drivers to see if you would enjoy it. They keep a large wall schedule of drivers on duty during the week. During your rounds, you are guaranteed some grateful smiles and thanks in return for your service.

There is another agency with similar goals called "Wheels To Meals" in which the driver picks up shut-ins and brings them to a central location where a meal is ready for them. The idea is to provide a social outing with people to chat with, and perhaps provide some free entertainment as well as a meal.

Project Four—Support a Charity or Church Bazaar

Local charities and church organizations usually have one or two fundraising sales events during the year to raise tax-exempt revenue either for the church needs or charitable causes in your community. The events may be called church bazaars, tea and bake sales, craft sales, fall fairs, or orange or peach festivals. The goal of the event is to raise money through the sale of items that are often both created and sold by a group of volunteer workers. Participation in these events may require creative and organizational effort and can be highly sociable.

Most churches have a women's auxiliary, a group of fifteen to twenty church members, who are responsible for the social aspects of after-service functions. Typically, they prepare tea, sandwiches, and cookies for parishioners to munch on while they socialize after the weekly church service. This same group also participates in two to three annual fundraising events in which they prepare saleable foodstuffs, such as fudge brownies or chocolate chip cookies, or decorative crafts, such as door or table ornaments. Retirees who have a flair for baking or for making unique crafts will enjoy these highly social groups.

Nonreligious community charities, such as the Kiwanis Club, the United Way, the Rotary Club, and the March of Dimes need volunteers to help them with their annual and varied fund raising events. Most towns and cities have seen the growth of food banks in the past twenty years, which accept donations of food from individuals, other charities, and supermarkets. These food banks are staffed by volunteers who help to sort and repackage cans and boxes of food into boxed rations for low-income groups. Typically, volunteers in urban food banks are of all ages and from all different cultures.

If you think you would enjoy volunteering your time, you might consider consulting the yellow pages of your telephone directory under "Social Service Organizations." You may be surprised at the variety of agencies that function in your area, including the Salvation Army, Assault Trauma Centers, Bereavement Counseling, and Seniors' Outreach Services. Keep in mind that some agencies are better equipped to train and work with volunteers than others. Your talents and energy are valuable. Shop around until you find a place that seems to appreciate your efforts.

Project Five—Visit a Shut-In

Shut-ins: every residential street and every apartment building has them at some time. These are the single or widowed people who because of an infirmary, such as poor eyesight, crippling arthritis, or a broken hip, or because of a loss of income or loss of the use of their car, are no longer able to do the simple tasks that life demands. What they need most is a friend to give them a helping hand, perhaps once a week.

One of the key roles that a volunteer might play is to contact the various agencies on behalf of the shut-in to make sure that those services are being provided. Rather than being the service provider themselves, volunteer visitors can teach clients to be as independent as possible by using existing community services geared to help them. If the disability is substantial, there are some social agencies that can assist the housebound person, including "Meals On Wheels," which can provide a hot meal once a day delivered to their door, home-care nursing to provide periodic medical checkups, and a transportation service for disabled and wheelchair-bound clients. In addition, some commercial outlets, such as pharmacies, grocery stores, and fast-food outlets, will deliver items to the person's residence.

Once the basic needs are cared for, the volunteer can then act as a friend to expand the client's social needs by reading to them, chatting about family, driving them to the doctors, to a store to shop for a gift, to the library, or taking them for a stroll in a park. Just getting out of the house once a week can be a great treat to someone who finds the four walls closing in on them.

When visiting them, listen carefully to what their specific needs are, and follow up on what can be done to help them.

Helping out a close relative or a neighbor that you have known for some time is relatively easy. But if you are a complete stranger to a neighbor, trust becomes an issue and help may be rejected. Volunteers might consider working through a church committee that reaches out to shut-ins, or through a relative's referral. In all cases, offer assistance a little at a time to ensure trust and acceptance of your help. After all, it's their life, not yours. They still have to learn to accept their new disability and the loss of part of their independence—something that is not easy to learn.

Gifts that might be welcomed by shut-ins include potted plants, flowers, freshly baked cookies or pastries, birthday cards, batteries for their television remote, video or DVD rentals, a smile, and a cheerful attitude.

Project Six—Wrap Gifts For Charity

One seasonal way to help others is to volunteer as one of the Christmas gift wrappers who appear in shopping malls three to four weeks before Christmas. You may have seen their rectangular formation of tables cluttered with wrapping paper, ribbons, bows, scotch tape, and scissors located near a mall entrance in the center of the walkway. This giftwrapping service is actually a fundraising event for local charities who use the profits to help the handicapped, visually impaired, or other special-needs groups in the community. So, when you donate your time to this service, you help to support a charity, as well as assist time-constrained or klutzy customers who know they need help with wrapping their presents.

There are several advantages to this type of volunteering. One is that it's seasonal; another is that the giftwrapping skills are easy to learn. Most wrappers use the same techniques on all presents. Their biggest challenge is how to wrap the odd shapes, such as a flower vase, a table lamp, or tool kit. Often, the solution is to resort to boxing the item first before attempting to wrap it, or suggesting that the customer use a Christmas bag stuffed with colored tissue paper as an alternative. These wrapping stations usually have various size boxes and decorative bags for sale as well. Another advantage is that you can pick your hours to volunteer. The mall might be open from 9:00 A.M. to 9:00 P.M. and the wrapping desk volunteers appear in shifts. Retired people often show up in the mornings and afternoons, whereas volunteers getting off work from another job often take the evening shift.

If this type of activity appears interesting, contact someone at one of the wrapping desks and ask how you can become a volunteer wrapper. There is usually one person who is in charge of organizing and scheduling these wrapping stations and who may look after several shopping malls simultaneously. Talk to that person. Tell them you are retired and interested in volunteering your time at a particular location, during a particular part of the day. Pick a mall close to home.

As a final thought, there's something rewarding about interacting with customers and helping a charity simultaneously. It's a great mood lifter. You get to practice your best smile, chat with people, and whistle Christmas tunes while pretending that you are one of Santa's little helpers. You may even dare to wear a Santa's hat, a Christmas badge, or a special Christmas tie to put people at ease. Why not? It's a fun, charitable time of the year.

Creative Retirement

Project Seven—Volunteer at the Seniors' Center

Most communities have a Seniors' Activity Center, a nonprofit civic organization operated for the benefit of active seniors in that area. They host social events, exercise classes, workshops, seminars, craft classes, and group trips for their members. Except for one or two permanent employees, the activities of the organization are entirely planned and operated by volunteer members. Volunteers play a variety of roles, which include teaching, organizing and hosting special events, communications, and planning.

People volunteer as craft instructors, providing classes in how to embroider, crochet, paint watercolors, do bunka art, decorate clothing, solder glass, arrange flowers, cook, and use a computer for e-mail and word processing. Workshop instructors are also required for teaching t'ai chi, stretching classes, and dance classes. Seminar leaders, those people who give information in the form of a lecture or interactive sessions, are required for topics like the best holidays for seniors, keeping healthy, flower and vegetable gardening, understanding investments, poetry readings, and researching family histories.

Volunteers also organize and host special events at the seniors' center. Primarily they decorate, assemble chairs and tables, provide refreshments, and cook and serve meals for the members. Decorations are often part of special celebrations such as St. Patrick's Day, Valentine's Day, and Halloween. Some organizations rent their facilities for birthdays, wedding anniversary celebrations, and dances, and the seniors volunteer as beverage and food hosts.

Members can also volunteer as communication specialists in the organization, designing and printing a monthly upcoming events newsletter on the computer, in addition to keeping the activities bulletin board up to date with notices, congratulations, and photographs. Members are also needed to design and update tournament schedules for card games, chess matches, and outside golfing excursions.

Center activities are thought up by its own members based on interest surveys and member recommendations. To get these activities started, an executive committee of volunteers get together with a chairperson, and the details of the event are discussed, researched, and decided upon. Examples of committee topics include which workshops and seminars will be offered, destinations of group day trips, and which special events will be honored. Some beginning executive committees also debate and publish the overall goals of the organization in the form of an organizational constitution. Additional activity groups focus on one specific task, such as providing a workshop or a banquet for the members.

Project Eight—Help the Humane Society

If the big brown eyes of an injured Labrador retriever or the cries of a newborn orphaned kitten tug at your heart strings, the Humane Society may be an attractive volunteer organization worth considering. This group looks after abused, neglected, and abandoned animals in your community. They also perform surgery on animals who have had injuries, such as owls with broken wings, or squirrels and raccoons with broken legs or bruised heads from car or tree accidents. Humane Society volunteers help nurse these critters back to health before releasing them back into their habitats.

Volunteers are welcomed in a number of capacities like watching over animals that are getting exercise while briefly out of their cages, helping with daily feedings, and keeping the cages clean and tidy. Some handling tasks include dog walking, dog grooming, cat grooming, and bottle feeding of infant pets. Abused and neglected animals have a past history of poor treatment from humans and tend to back away from an extended hand. Some volunteers specialize in getting animals to trust humans once again. They usually concentrate their efforts on one or two animals at a time as they talk gently to them, feed them, pet them, groom them, and take them for walks. Most of the animals begin to respond positively to abuse-recovery therapy and are then suitable to be put up for adoption.

Other volunteers offer clerical services by answering telephone inquiries, looking after semiannual mailings to local households, and getting involved in fund raising activities to raise awareness of the efforts of the organization, which persuades people to donate money to its operation. Some organizations bring pets to display at shopping malls, fairs, and conventions to encourage pet adoptions. Some do "show and tell" at elementary schools to teach youngsters the correct methods of caring for home pets. Education about pet population control through neutering, transmissible diseases like rabies, and typical pet afflictions, such as arthritis, dental problems, and intestinal worms and fleas, are often shared through conference brochures, school workshops, and mailings to Humane Society members. Overall, the Humane Society is a worthwhile organization, which acts as an advocate on behalf of a group that has no voice of its own. Animals learn that some humans are humane and do care about them.

Project Nine—Be a Food Bank Volunteer

Despite a thriving economy and reports of successful welfare reform stories, twenty-six million Americans recently sought emergency food assistance from Second Harvest, America's largest collection of food banks, plus an additional ten million Americans turned to Catholic Charities, Inc., the nation's largest charity organization for food assistance. These organizations collect and distribute food to grassroots agencies, such as community centers, soup kitchens, food pantries, shelters, seniors' programs, and childcare centers. These organizations have noted a 10 percent rise in use each year for the past ten years. The largest user groups are children and seniors.

Retirees are welcomed by both the collection organizations and the myriad of food service agencies. Volunteer jobs may include driving vans and stacking and sorting food in the warehouses. Farmers and ranchers whose crops and livestock were devastated by floods or droughts, are often limited to one- or two-week supplies of food each month at local church food pantries. Canned goods, flour, peanut butter, and dry boxed food, such as cereal and macaroni mix, are the most durable of the sorted products.

The urban food service agencies, such as soup kitchens, food pantries, and community centers, offer a greater variety of volunteer roles, including food preparation, serving meals, cleanup crews, drivers for "Meals On Wheels," meal planners, staff schedulers, maintenance crew and in some cases, background entertainers.

Retirees seeking to volunteer their services should check the yellow pages of the phone book under Volunteer Service Agencies, or the Help Wanted section of a local newspaper. Talk to other retirees about their experiences in similar volunteer capacities. Chat with a parish priest or the manager of a local agency about part-time openings. Choose a neighborhood agency that best appreciates your efforts and benefits people in your community. Also bring a smile. It's inexpensive as well as a morale booster for people who need it most.

Project Ten—Run For Charity

Each spring and summer, towns and cities typically organize a Run for Charity event in which participants agree to walk or run a five or ten-mile downtown route as a charity fund raiser. Sample charities may include breast cancer research, Multiple Sclerosis Foundation, and the Kidney Foundation. The advertisements for the events usually appear in the local newspaper and on the local radio station. After signing up at sponsoring retailers, each participant is responsible for finding people who will sponsor them as a walker or jogger by pledging to donate $0.25 to $2.00 for each mile/kilometre that the participant successfully completes. The greater the number of signed-up sponsors, the greater the amount of money earned for the charity.

Active retirees find these events invigorating because they are not competitive, nor are they subject to time constraints. There are also no rules for completing the whole route. Joggers can quit anytime and get their distance verified. Even elderly retirees can participate with a slow-paced jog. The route has support staff along the way with bottled water and medical assistance, if required. Some athletes enter as sponsored wheelchair participants. Joggers can bring headphones and audiotapes to keep them distracted and motivated. The entire event may last four hours from start to finish.

It is recommended, however, that participants practice a few weeks before the event by walking several miles a day to develop stamina, as well as a sense of how far they are capable of jogging or walking in a single session. It's also a good idea to obtain a comfortable pair of running shoes and extra socks to cushion the impact on hard pavement and to avoid getting blisters. A light short-sleeved top and shorts are typical jogging attire. A baseball cap and sunglasses may also be needed on bright sunny days. A walk in the sun to help others? Not a bad way to spend a day.

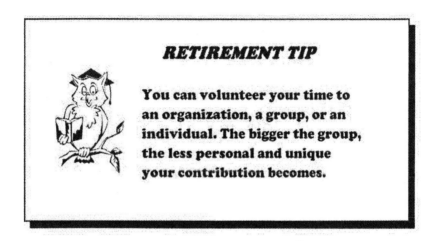

RETIREMENT TIP

You can volunteer your time to an organization, a group, or an individual. The bigger the group, the less personal and unique your contribution becomes.

Chapter Twelve

Projects For Nature Lovers

Nature lovers would rather be outside close to nature than doing other activities. They enjoy fishing, hunting, sailing, camping, skiing, ski-dooing, golfing, and anything else that takes them outdoors to experience the elements of nature—the climate, open skies, birds, animals, woodlands, streams, and the freshness of the air away from polluted, congested cities. They enjoy being one with nature. Check off the projects in this chapter that you might like doing.

Projects in This Chapter: ✔

1. Attend a Motorcycle Rally ☐
2. Cross-Country Camping - Couples ☐
3. Cross-Country Camping - Singles ☐
4. Vacation in a Motorhome ☐
5. Become a Golfer ☐
6. Go on an Adventure Tour ☐
7. Take Up Bird Watching ☐
8. Try Nature Photography ☐
9. Become a Flower Gardener ☐
10. Vacation on a Houseboat ☐

Project One—Attend a Motorcycle Rally

An interesting option for the motorcycle enthusiast is traveling to annual rallies in North America and enjoying their week-long activities. This middle-class phenomenon, unique to North America and particularly popular in the United States, has attracted thousands of people from all walks of life—urban professionals, factory workers, country farmers, and retired folk.

These are not members of a gang, but weekend hobby enthusiasts who love the outdoors and enjoy riding across the country on their Honda, Indian, Yamaha, or Harley-Davidson road cruisers, sometimes with a sidecar, most of the time with a spouse or partner hanging on behind the rider. They meet in Burbank, California, Pigeon Forge, Tennessee, and the Lake George area of New York state for annual reunions. Harley-Davidson bikers were treated to a huge celebration in Milwaukee, Wisconsin, recently for the manufacturer's anniversary. When these motorcycle enthusiasts take off their helmets to reveal greying hair and bifocals, you realize that there are a great number of retirees enjoying the camaraderie of these well-organized events.

One of the larger gatherings suited to retirees is called Americade, which is held in June in the Adirondack resort area near Lake George in New York state. About fifty thousand like-minded souls of all ages get together and stay in hotels, or tents, to witness the nonstop action. Some stay at Bolton's Landing about ten miles away. Attendees are entertained in large conference centers with a number of events: precision drill-team demonstrations, motorcycle calf roping, fashion shows, oldest and youngest rider competitions, night-time bike motorcades, live band entertainment, and fireworks. The resort areas also offer lake cruises, para-sailing, and excellent inns and restaurants.

The Pigeon Forge gathering is next to the Dollywood Theme Park and the Dixie Rodeo complex. There are lots of major hotels for accommodation, but booking rooms six months to a year in advance is advisable. There are also specific-event bike rallies such as the Celebrity Bikeathon in California that talk show host Jay Leno, among others, enjoys participating in, and various Ride for Charity events.

Talk to other bikers in person or in Internet chat rooms about such events and get their opinions and suggestions. For additional information contact:

Americade
Box 2205
Glen Falls, New York 12801
Website: www.tourexpo.com

Project Two—Cross-Country Camping—Couples

If you are a person who enjoys the smell of fresh air, loves to see the beauty of the wilderness, and enjoys a leisurely, quiet pace, you might consider cross-country camping. This inexpensive method of travel involves the use of organized campgrounds and state or provincial parks instead of motels for overnight stays. Two factors have greatly improved outdoor camping in the past decade. The first factor is the growth of a network of privately owned full-service campgrounds to supplement the existing state-run parks. The second factor is an expanded choice of mobile living conditions for traveling families, which include tenting, sleeper vans, small trailers, mobile homes, and motorhomes. Over sixty-four million Americans have made outdoor camping one of the most popular hobbies in the United States.

One of the major private campground providers is The Kampgrounds of America, Inc. (KOA), which has hundreds of family-owned franchised sites in the United States and Canada. Most KOA sites offer vacationers three modes of camping (average costs based on two adults): tent site $20/night; RV campsite with water, electricity, and sewer hookups for mobile trailers or motorhomes $25/night; one-room log cabin (bring your own sleeping bag and pillows) $35/night. All campgrounds offer centralized rest rooms, individual shower facilities, coin laundries, picnic tables, and a full-service variety store. Several offer on-site tennis, badminton, swimming, fishing, and canoeing, or are close to major entertainment or shopping centers that you can drive to. KOA also publishes an inexpensive annual *Road Atlas and Camping Guide* with specific prices and easy-to-follow directions to their campgrounds.

Another annual publication that provides data on both private and state-run campgrounds and RV parks is *Woodall's North American Campground Directory,* which also rates the maintenance and quality of services available at the sites on a scale from one to five. This 700-page reference includes directional maps, evaluated write-ups on approximately fifteen thousand campsites, and campground advertisements similar to yellow page listings, usually positioned next to the write ups. The book is organized alphabetically by state and province and is easy to read. For more information on campgrounds, you may wish to consult the following references.

Woodall Publication Corp.
13975 West Polo Trail Drive
Lake Forest, Illinois
60045-5000
Toll-Free: 1-800-323-9076
Website: www.woodalls.com

This company publishes the *Woodall's North American Campground Directory,* which is the RVers bible for locating and comparing campgrounds in the United States and Canada. Explains costs and amenities and provides maps. Also available in bookstores in the spring.

KOA Kampgrounds Directory
Road Atlas and Camping Guide
Kampgrounds of America, Inc.
Executive Offices

Billings, Montana 59114-0558
Phone: 1-406-248-7444

This directory covers KOA franchises for the United States and Canada. Describes campsite facilities and provides road atlas. Available in the bookstores in the spring.

California Camping: The Complete Guide to More Than 50,000 Campsites
by Tom Stienstra Foghorn Printers, 1998
ISBN 1573540056

Popular reference for campers seeking getaways in California, particularly in the state parks.

Project Three—Cross-Country Camping—Singles

Retirees who are single or whose partner has passed away often feel lost without a companion to share the experiences of traveling. If you are in that position, you might find inspiration from the fifty-six-year-old author, lecturer, and solo world traveler Joei Carleton Hossack. She advises singles to follow their dreams and set off on their own travels.

Joei lost her husband on a retirement dream trip in 1992 while camping in Europe. Two years later to overcome her grief, she set off on annual solo travels and began writing about her experiences and publishing them. One of her books is titled *Kiss This, Florida, I'm Outa Here.* To date, she has four books in print and uses her book royalties to finance her excursions. In 1998, she became a full-time RVer with a pickup truck sleeper camper. She has taken solo trips to Turkey, the Greek Islands, and Cyprus. She has also driven solo in her camper truck from Florida to Alaska and has volunteered at archeological digs in the south of England.

She says women often have the idea that they have to have someone to be with to enjoy traveling. "I don't think like that," she tells people at her book signings. "If you want to do something, go out and do it. Wherever I go, I make friends and have lots of fun." She offers several tips for traveling on your own. Don't travel at night. Drive 160-200 kilometres in one day and stay at each location for a week. "Compared to my husband, I was a couch potato. Now I'm discovering how gutsy I am."

If you are not brave enough to try Joei's camper approach to travel, you might consider the more expensive escorted tours for single travelers. There are several travel companies that design both educational world tours as well as outdoor experience packages for the single traveler. These small group excursions include an experienced tour guide who handles all the bookings for accommodations, transportation, and recommendations for things to see and places to eat. As a single person, you will be absorbed into the group as you travel with them.

For additional information on solo traveling, refer to the following sources.

Restless from the Start
by Joei Carlton Hossack
Skeena Press, 1997
ISBN 0965750906

Everyone's Dream, Everyone's Nightmare
by Joei Carlton Hossack
Skeena Press 1998
ISBN 0965750914

ADDITIONAL RESOURCES FOR
WOMEN TRAVELING ALONE

The Women's Travel Club, Inc.
21401 NE 38th Avenue
Aventura, Florida 33180
Phone: 1-800-480-4448
Fax: 305-937-7649
e-mail: womantrip@AOL.com
Website: www.womenstravelclub.com

An escorted group travel club for women only, which offers 25-30 group trips per year. Generally first class accommodations with professional guide on tours. Single or shared rooms. Annual membership fee. Club organizes the itinerary. Expensive, but they also do discount cruises and spa trips.

Senior Women's Travel
Mary Ann Zimmerman
Stanton Associates
136 East 56th Street
New York, NY 10022
Phone: 212-838-4740
Fax: 212-826-8710
E-mail: maryann@poshnosh.com
Website: www.poshnosh.com

Company offers no hassle, comfortable travel with itineraries that let you feel the heart and soul of the place. Everyone has their own room. Destinations include Venice, Paris, London, New York City, as well as exotic locations. Also grandmother and granddaughter excursions.

Traveling Solo Advice and Ideas for
More Than 250 Great Vacations
by Eleanor Berman
The Globe Pequot Press, 1999, 2nd Edition
ISBN 0762704187

Award-winning guide with advice for being single within a travel group. Chapters for women traveling alone, single parents, and older travelers. Lots of information on tours, resorts, and cruises.

Project Four—Vacation in a Motorhome

A growing phenomenon in vacationing and alternative lifestyles is the motorized version of a mobile home commonly referred to as a "motorhome." These extended truck-frame vehicles contain the same luxury elements of home living as the mobile trailer, except they include their own engine and driver's cab area.

The motorhome offers a distinct on-the-road lifestyle for retired couples who enjoy extended road trips all across North America combined with overnight stays in inexpensive campsites. No more packing and unpacking your suitcases. Your home, hobbies, and belongings all travel with you. Many retirees spend up to six months of the year away from home, seeking warm southern states in the winter and returning to their primary residence in the summer months. Other retirees use this recreational vehicle for overnight stays on specific sightseeing trips, such as vacations to Disney World, Dollywood, Busch Gardens, the Grand Canyon, or Niagara Falls. Some prefer a leisurely pace and seek out favorite hobbies and interests, such as arts and crafts shows, antique fairs, musical and dramatic performances, museums, historical sites, and sporting events, wherever they travel.

Motorhomes are supported all across the United States and Canada by a network of RV (recreational vehicle) trailer parks that provide individual motorhome sites with water, electricity, and sewer hookups that average about $25/night. Some campsites offer monthly rates for long-term stays for the intrepid "snowbirds."

Motorhomes can vary anywhere from ten to twelve feet wide, and sixteen to thirty-two feet long and typically contain a functional kitchen, dining table, washroom, shower, closets, master bedroom, television, VCR/DVD player, and captain's chairs for the front two seats. Some even have a back-mounted camera to view traffic following the motorhome. Prices vary by size and can range from $50,000 to $200,000. One publication that evaluates all types of recreational vehicles is *Woodall's RV Buyer's Guide.*

The advantage of the motorhome over a comparable size trailer-type mobile home is that it is easier to manoeuvre, the engine is matched to its pull weight, and the entire interior of the vehicle can be accessed while in motion, which lends itself to a wide range of activities for the nondriving partner or additional passengers.

The disadvantages of a motorhome are low gas mileage and a nondetachable driving section for scooting into town for shopping, replenishing supplies, and sightseeing. Some vacationers attach a compact car with a tow bar to the back of the motorhome to provide more flexibility. Be forewarned, though, both trailer-type mobile homes and motor homes depreciate in resale value fairly rapidly when compared to an ordinary house or cottage, which tends to increase in value over time. If you are unsure whether or not you will enjoy the motorhome experience, consider renting one for a summer before making a purchase. Look for RV rentals in the telephone book. For additional information, you may wish to refer to the following sources.

*The RVer's Bible: Everything You Need to Know
About Choosing, Using, and Enjoying Your RV*
by Kim Baker, and Sunny Baker
Fireside Publishers, 1997
ISBN 0684822679

Excellent guide to living and traveling in a recreational vehicle. Chapters on purchasing, maintaining the rig, and navigating the emotional pitfalls of life on the road. Humorous, popular reference.

RVing Basics
by Bill Moeller
McGraw-Hill Publishers, 1995
ISBN 0070427798

Practical, comprehensive guide for novice RVer's. Topics includes choosing an appropriate vehicle, considering various interior options, what to expect at RV campground sites, and cleaning and maintaining the vehicle.

*Living Aboard Your RV: A Guide to the
Fulltime Life on Wheels*
by Janet Groene and Gordon Groene
Tab Books, 1993, 2nd Edition
ISBN 0877423407

Inexpensive, easy-to-read RV guide. Topics include choosing your home on wheels, house cleaning, security, repairs, and maintenance. Realistic portrait of life on the road.

Project Five—Become a Golfer

One of the most popular and enduring outdoor activities for retirees over the past fifty years is the sport of golfing. No other retirement endeavor has as many Internet websites or as much television coverage as this particular sport. It is played on every continent with the exception of Antarctica. It is played by amateurs and professionals of all age groups. There are inexpensive public golf courses that can be enjoyed by all at reasonable daily rates of $30, or annual rates of $300 to $500, and exclusive high-priced private golf courses for those who can afford the exorbitant membership fees that can range from $5,000 to $25,000 a year.

If you have never played, golf is a sport that requires skill, patience, and plenty of practice. Having a sense of humor also helps. Many golfers describe it as an addictive sport because of its intermittent "great day" experiences that keep participants coming back.

The best way to learn golf is to hire a golf instructor. Instructors are usually available at golf courses and provide group or private lessons for a fee. Some getaway golf resorts cater to the novices who wish to immerse themselves in the sport. There are also numerous independent driving ranges for practicing your long shot and interesting and fun putting courses for practicing short distance putts. Also books and videos can help teach golfing techniques.

There are a number of one-time expenses for novice golfers, including the purchase of a set of clubs, golf bag, golf balls, golf shoes, and golfing attire. Clubs come in different lengths for people of varying heights, and are designed for right or left-handed individuals. It is recommended that you rent clubs when first starting to test them out, and then get professional advice in golf club selection from a golf pro shop rather than a sports store salesperson.

Most sports shops that cater to golfers offer a range of clothing for men and women. There are also a number of fixed and variable costs for each outing, including an annual membership fee, green fees for each game (sometimes waived for annual members), pull-cart rentals, or motorized golf cart rentals for those who prefer not to walk, and optional clubhouse expenses such as drinks and light meals. A typical one-day outing may cost $40 to $60, not including meals, drinks, and lost golf balls.

You can go to the golf course alone and sign up for the next available group of four people. You can also go with a group of friends and golf together. After a while, most people develop favorite golf partners who tend to meet at the same time for a round of golf. A round of golf can be a short game of nine holes or a full game of eighteen holes, which usually requires four hours to complete.

There are some unwritten rules of golf course etiquette. If you are in a beginner's group or with a group of slow players, always allow a faster team behind you to *play through*, which means allowing them to tee off ahead of you. They will be out of sight in no time. Also, green fees are needed because tufts of grass referred to as *divots* are thrown into the air when you swing your golf club. Replace your divots if you can find them, and press them into place with your foot to help them take root again. A third rule of etiquette is not to speak, whistle, or make noise when another golfer is swinging. Doing so is considered rude and a vulgar display of bad manners. Making disparaging remarks after some else's bad swing is also considered rude.

The great advantage of the sport of golf is its portability. It is available in your home town, near most retirement communities, and near most cities where you are on vacation. Husband and wife teams, in particular, often enjoy golfing vacations in warmer climates during the winter and golfing at their local hometown golf course in the summer months. If you enjoy the outdoors, the grasslands of the nearest golf course may just become your favorite stomping grounds. As a sport, golf is challenging enough, yet gentle enough to be played for a lifetime.

Golf for Dummies
by McCord, Huggan, and Cooper
IDG Books Worldwide, 1999, 2nd Edition
ISBN 0764551469

Highly rated, humorous reference for beginning golfers. Topics include descriptions and uses of golf clubs, how to hit the ball, handling yourself on the green, rules, scoring. Photos of golf swings included.

Ben Hogan's Five Lessons: The
Modern Fundamentals of Golf
by Ben Hogan, and Sidney L. James
Simon and Schuster, 1989
ISBN 0671612972

Hardcover reprint of the classic golf reference. Hogan believes that the average golfer is entirely capable of achieving a score of 80 using methods described in his book.

Fodor's Golf Digest's Places to Play
by Fodor's Editors
Fodor's Travel Publications, 1998, 4th Edition
ISBN 0679034021

Great reference for the avid golfer and traveler. Describes the highest rated golf facilities as selected by readers of *Golf Digest* magazine. Lists 5,000 golf courses in the United States, Canada, Mexico, and the Caribbean.

Golf Resorts of the World: The Best Places to Stay
by McCallen, McAllen, and Klemme
Harry N. Abrams Publisher, 1993
ISBN 0810933721

For golfers with no financial restrictions, this reference rates and profiles golfs resorts from around the world. Includes accommodations. restaurants, and other available amenities. 402 full-color photographs.

The Legend of Bagger Vance
VHS/DVD 2000
ASIN: B00005AAB9

This inspirational, mystical golf movie and love story is set in early 1930s Savannah, Georgia and will appeal to the noncompetitive golfer. Stars Matt Damon, Charlize Theron, and Will Smith.

Creative Retirement

Project Six—Go on an Adventure Tour

Adventure tours are vacations that often involve a certain level of physical activity and are generally aimed at retirees who are still physically fit. Travel agents also package these specialized vacations for those travelers who want a different type of experience on their holidays. These trips are not designed for those who want to enjoy the view from the window of a tour bus, or for those who want to stay in a five-star hotel and lounge by the swimming pool.

Expect to be walking, hiking, back packing, or bike riding. The type of activity and level of fitness required are usually identified in the catalogs or travel brochures. Travel agents target the seniors' market with the lower-activity, slower-paced vacations. It is not uncommon to find seniors in their sixties and seventies on leisurely bike tours in nature settings or on walking tours in the northern English countryside.

Adventure tours often use offbeat, out-of-the-way locations, such as intercity bike trails, national parks, or the quieter country roads. Travel destinations may be domestic or international, and they go beyond the traditional sightseeing packages to allow travelers to experience the countryside rather than to drive through it. There are a number of travel agencies that concentrate on adventure tours for the over-fifty crowd.

ElderTreks
Website: www.eldertreks.com

Advertised as the world's first adventure company dedicated to people fifty and over. Their escorted worldwide travel destinations include many exotic locations, such as China, Australia, New Zealand, Africa, Queen Charlotte Islands, Tibet, and Thailand. Tours are typically small groups of sixteen people and involve walking, biking, and some hiking in rainforest, desert, or mountainous environments. Travelers participate in the diverse cultures by strolling through markets, and eating local dishes, and talking to native people. Be prepared to walk for several hours at a comfortable pace under tropical conditions.

Adventure Quest
Telephone: 1-800-643-5630.
Website: www.adventurequest.com

Fourteen hundred adventures, voyages, and unique travel for individuals, families, and groups. Trips range from safaris, biking trips, and language classes abroad to hiking treks, nature expeditions, and rafting journeys. They have virtually all types of travel packages including animal treks, bicycling, cultural tours, fishing expeditions, nature or eco-tours, paddling, summer schools for seniors, skiing, golfing, aerial tours, arctic cruises, and water sports. They have a well-designed website with multiple options of tour type and worldwide destinations. The company also customizes slower-paced adventure holidays for less active seniors who are looking for a different kind of holiday.

All Florida Adventure Tours
Telephone: 1-800-33-Tour-3
Fax: allfla@aol.com
Website: www.all-florida-ecotours.com

Miami-based ground tour operator that specializes in customizing group and private tours for seniors who have particular hobby interests such as nature, bird watching, local history, art, photography, and fossil hunting. They also organize general interest group tours. The food and accommodations can be adjusted for the budget-minded or the more luxury-minded traveler.

Colorado Vacation Guide
Website: www.coloradoadventure.net

Adventure tours featuring bed and breakfasts, campgrounds, mountain lodging, dude ranches, horseback riding, and hunting and fishing.

Travel Unlimited: Uncommon Adventures for the Mature Traveler
by Alison Gardner
Avalon Travel Publishing, 2000
ISBN 1-56691-212-1

A unique book offering a worldwide menu of alternative travel adventures for older vacationers. Detailed reviews of ecological and cultural experiences ranging from the primitive to the luxurious.

Adventure New England: An Outdoor Vacation Guide
By Diane Blair, and Pamela Wright
McGraw-Hill Ryerson, Ltd. 1996
ISBN 0070033099

This guide offers 77 adventure vacations throughout New England which includes canoeing, sailing, fishing, and hot air ballooning. Information provided on rates, locations, and what to bring with you.

Project Seven—Take Up Bird Watching

There are nine thousand different species of birds in the world. The smallest is the bee hummingbird, which weighs less than three grams and is only found in Cuba. The world's largest bird is the flightless Australian ostrich, which may stand eight feet (2.5 meters) tall and weight three hundred pounds (135 kilograms).

North America is home to more than eight hundred species of birds. This is a daunting number for a beginning bird watcher who is merely trying to identify a feathered visitor at a backyard feeder. But the task is easier than it seems. Most indigenous birds are regional in habitat and, along with a few migratory critters who like to go south for the winter, only a few dozen varieties will actually live in a particular area at any one time. As a result, bird watching, sometimes referred to as birding, is enjoyed by millions of hobbyists. The challenge is not only finding these skittish and elusive creatures, but also accurately identifying each bird seen.

There are a number of excellent bird watching reference guides, such as the *Field Guide to the Birds of North America* published by the National Geographic Society. They contain color renditions of each bird, along with detailed descriptions of appearance, habitat, and feeding patterns to assist the hobbyist with location and identification.

To make your hobby more interesting, you might consider using a checklist to record your encounters with birds. The back of most field guides has checklists for that purpose. Some hobbyists record their sightings in a small portable notebook. To turn the hobby into a social outing, birders might consider joining a local bird watching club. They take frequent field trips to various areas, and their combined enthusiasm can make the hobby quite addictive.

Another variation of the hobby is to become a bird photographer. You can snap close-ups of different birds capturing their various colors and shapes using a single-lens reflex 35mm film or digital camera with a 100-300mm telephoto zoom lens. The photos can then be framed and mounted on a wall or inserted into a bird photo album with labels and descriptions. You might even consider transferring digitized images into a computer, then organizing them on a regional bird watching website that you set up to assist other hobbyists who are using the Internet to do some background research. For additional information on this interesting hobby, refer to the following bird watching websites.

Birdzilla
www.Birdzilla.com

Find out how to cultivate a bird oasis in your backyard and how to identify the various birds that drop in for a bite or bath.

Backyard Birding
www.bcpl.net

The Baltimore Bird Club has gathered a list of do's and don'ts, along with additional information on establishing hummingbird and butterfly gardens, and building birdhouses.

BirdSource
www.birdsource.cornell.edu

Cornell University and the Audubon Society bird count maps showing where various types of birds are concentrated in North America. Also describes the songs of some birds which are difficult to identify by markings alone.

Project Eight—Try Nature Photography

If you love both the outdoors and taking pictures, you might consider becoming a naturalist photographer— someone who captures the beauty of scenic landscapes, waterfalls, rivers, mountains, animals, and birds in pictures. Some concepts worth studying are backdrop scenes, foreground subjects, and animate and inanimate objects, and type of lens best suited for the task.

To be a good nature photographer it helps to think of yourself as a painter painting a canvas. Like a painter, you have to be concerned with the background of the scene and also provide a foreground subject for the viewer to focus on. Winding rivers, white-water rapids, waterfalls, and ocean shorelines make excellent backdrops for nature photographs. Distant mountains, particularly those with snowcapped peaks, are also visually pleasing. Professional nature photographers look for these backgrounds, then choose a subject to place in the foreground for the viewer to focus on. For example, suppose you're using a rocky ocean coastline as your background. Suitable foreground subjects might include fishing boats tied to a dock, or a lonely lighthouse placed left or right of center in the shot, or a close-up of a bearded old man in a turtleneck sweater looking out to sea.

Another example might be an early morning scene with a large lake, bordered by trees and with mountains in the background. In the shallows of the lake, just off to the side, a moose feeding off aquatic vegetation raises his head to look at you. Or the same scene with a bear and her cubs at the shoreline for a morning drink, or

247

a beautiful blue jay sitting on a bare branch near the shore. A regular 50mm lens is suitable for these shots because it keeps both the background and foreground in focus at the same time.

Be forewarned, though. Inanimate objects like boats, lobster nets, docks, and lighthouses do not move and will wait with endless patience while you compose your shot in your camera's viewfinder. Animate objects, such as moose, deer, and birds, tend to move around at their own pace and will require much faster reaction times on your part. Mama bears with newborn cubs can be particularly uncooperative. A camera option called a motor-driven film advance is recommended for a rapid series of shots when photographing animals—along with a clear escape route for quick getaways. Modern zoos with outdoor settings instead of cages provide safe locations for a variety of natural-looking photo shoots.

People can make great subjects if you get their cooperation. You might bring your own subject—a spouse, sibling, or offspring to pose for you against a beautiful background. A stranger might consider a five or ten dollar modeling fee suitable compensation for their fifteen minutes of time. If you plan to publish photos of people in the future, you need to get them to sign a photo release form, giving you permission to use them in publications. If the photo is for your wall or photo album, you need not bother.

A second approach to nature photography is to concentrate solely on the subject without worrying about the background. This is achieved by standing back several yards from the subject, using a zoom telephoto lens, filling the viewfinder with the subject, and taking the picture. This method puts the background out of focus while leaving only the bird, moose, squirrel, or raccoon as the only object in the photograph. If possible, focus the lens on the animal's eyes. When the eyes are clearly in focus, take the picture. It's the animal's eyes, not their tail or their spots that are key to capturing the essence of the subject. Eye contact with the animal in the photograph causes viewers to experience a brief sense of intimacy with a wild animal. Other great photos might include a close-up of a hummingbird in midair drinking nectar from a flower or a formation of baby ducks following behind their mother on land or in the water.

A third approach to nature photography is to experiment with macro lenses that provide extreme close-ups of objects. This is useful for photographing insects, tiny lizards, butterflies, and flowers. Macro lenses also throw the background out of focus, so adjusting the focus of the lens exactly on the object is critical to a successful photograph. Because you are photographing subjects in color, contrast is important in close-up work. A black beetle photographed against a dark green leaf is not going to look very distinct or interesting. However, an orange ladybug with black spots sitting on a white flower, with a drop of reflective dew on a nearby leaf, makes for excellent contrast and an interesting picture.

In addition to an artist's eye and technical skills with the camera, nature photography requires patience. Birds, insects, and mammals are not always ready for picture-taking when you are. Gorgeous sunsets scintillating off the water can add a dramatic effect to an ordinary photograph, but they disappear quickly and do not wait for you to compose the shot. Check the weather channel for sunrise and sunset times, if they are to be part of your composition, then sit with your camera ready before they occur. Great photographs are worth planning and waiting for. For further information, please refer to the following resources:

National Geographic Field Guide:
Secrets to Making Great Pictures
by Peter Burian, and Robert Caputo
National Geographic Society, 1999
ISBN   0792274989

A well-written glossy guide packed with beautiful color photos. The first half of the book covers the basics of photography. The second half covers a broad range of topics including people, animals, sports, architecture, and landscapes.

Professional Secrets of Nature
Photography: Essential Skills
for Photographing Outdoors
by Judy Holmes
Amherst Media, 2000
ISBN   1584280212

Tips on how to photograph flowers, landscapes, and wildlife, using natural light in varying weather conditions. Over 60 photographs included.

Project Nine—Become a Flower Gardener

Do you periodically sprout a green thumb? Do you feel a compulsion to get your hands into soil when signs of spring arrive? Maybe you suffer from the most common of home-owner's afflictions gardening fever. Gardening is a great way to add life and beauty to your home and property. Beds of flowers can accent your home and add color and vitality to an otherwise ho-hum front or back lawn.

Plants can be classified as either annual, biennial, or perennial. Annual plants live for only one growing season, during which they produce seeds, then die. Examples include petunias, marigolds, and Impatiens. Biennial plants, such as some types of foxglove, live for two growing seasons before setting seed and dying. The term perennial refers to plants that live longer than two years, such as daisies, blue veronicas, columbine, and songbird garden, and hanging basket favorites like lobelias and ivy leaf geraniums.

A garden involves annual chores to maintain its beauty. Seedlings must be purchased and planted and nurtured throughout the growing season. They need to be fertilized, watered, and protected from plant-eating bugs and invading weeds. All plants need certain things to survive—light, air, water, and mineral nutrients. As a gardener, your job is to ensure that all these needs are met. The warmer, drier, windier, and sunnier it is, the more water a plant loses to transpiration. During dry weather, this water must be replaced on a daily basis or the plants will wilt and die.

Garden soils vary from one location to another. Some are heavy clay, some are light and sandy, some are acidic, and so on. All of them contain bacteria and fungi, a few of which can cause problems for germinating seeds. Novice gardeners may have better success with soil-free, seed-starting mixes made from a mixture of peat, vermiculite, and perlite that has been sterilized to kill microorganisms. As the name implies, they contain no actual soil, but have a good balance between water retention and drainage, and may contain fertilizer. Purchasing potted seedlings that have already started growing in a local hothouse and have sprouted their own root systems provides a good head start for novice growers, over the traditional method of planting packaged dry flower seeds.

Chat with neighbors who have successful flower beds in your area and get their advice. Ask gardening supply retailers for what seems to work best in your particular climate. Read a book on basic gardening tips. Visit a website, such as Burpee.com, which has an online gardening school (flowers and vegetables) for beginners. The most informed gardeners have the prettiest and most successful flower beds. For additional information on flower gardening, refer to the following sources.

Burpee.com
www.Burpee.com

Burpee is an online supplier of seeds and gardening supplies. The website has an online course in gardening for beginners called Burpee Gardening School.

The Garden Gate
www. garden-gate.prairienet.org
This is a collection of horticultural sites around the world, including chat rooms, mail-order shopping, and teaching sites.

Home Gardening Tips
www.doityourself.com
This website contains nearly 100 articles on backyard gardening, landscaping, improving clay soils, compost, and indoor plants.

Better Homes and Gardens
Complete Guide to Flower Gardening
by Susan A. Roth
Better Homes & Gardens Books, 1995
ISBN 0696000571

A highly recommended book on flower gardening for beginners. Covers 450 plants and has 630 color photos, 100 illustrations, and 24 garden layout plans.

The Complete Idiot's Guide to Flower Gardening
by Mara Grey, and Kate Staples
MacMillan, 1999
ISBN 0028631404

Beginner's guide to flowers that are undemanding and generous. Contains 50 illustrations and a 16-page color insert.

Project Ten—Vacation on a Houseboat

Have you ever camped out on a lake in a houseboat? If you enjoy being on the water and traveling at a leisurely pace to see the sights, you might consider a vacation on a rented houseboat and spend one or two weeks during the summer cruising lakes, rivers, or canal systems. These floating motorhomes come complete with private bedrooms, bathrooms, kitchens, microwave ovens, fridges, cupboards, entertainment centers, open upper decks, and back patios. Larger models also have air conditioning, queen-size beds, full-size fridges, showers, propane barbecues, hot tubs, two bathrooms, couches, a sit-down bar, and oak kitchen tables that seat six people at a time.

Many vacation rental companies offer customers a choice of houseboats. Their dimensions resemble those of mobile trailers. Most are fifteen feet wide with lengths varying from thirty-five feet to eighty feet. Longer models have both increased space and more luxurious furniture and fixtures. Houseboats become more affordable if the cost is shared between two or three couples. Costs for two people are nearly comparable to ocean cruising. A mid-range model, seven-day rental in peak season (July and August) would cost one couple $3800, two couples $1900, three couples $1260 each. This includes rental, gas, and insurance, but not state taxes or food and beverage. You can also decrease the cost 10 percent by renting in the slightly cooler weather of late June or early September, or by 40 percent by vacationing in Canada and taking advantage of the exchange rates.

Houseboat renters typically cruise during the day, as well as fish, swim, chat, sunbathe, read novels, practice wildlife and nature photography, go ashore to explore waterfront towns or state parks, and enjoy the passing view. In the evenings, they can anchor the shallow craft on a beach or island or at a marina dock (where gas can be purchased) and watch indoor movies, play cards, assemble puzzles, and have an outdoor barbecue of grilled fish, steak, or hamburgers in the warm night air while watching a golden sunset reflect off the water. The houseboat is completely lighted with ceiling fixtures and table lamps for nighttime use. Agencies recommend that you anchor rather than cruise at night because of unseen water hazards.

There are Internet websites that allow you to select the vacation location by state or province. There are also houseboat rental companies in Canada, Australia, New Zealand, the Bahamas, Cuba, Belgium, England, and Ireland. Vacationers primarily interested in fishing should choose areas that cater to the sport and the type of fish that they enjoy eating. Those interested in warm weather might consider Arizona, California, Florida, or Texas as their houseboat vacation spot. For further information, please refer to the following sources.

Internet Websites
Website: www.houseboatingworld.com
Website: www.houseboatrentalcenter.com

Allows clients to select locations by country. Gives name of the lake, river or canal with houseboat rentals in each area. Also try keywords: Houseboat Vacations.

Houseboat (magazine)
Harris Publishing, Inc
Website: www.houseboatmagazine.com/

Monthly hobby magazine devoted to the lifestyle of houseboating. You can subscribe online. $44/yr.

Chapter Thirteen

Projects For the Athlete

The retired person who enjoys keeping physically fit tends to select noncompetitive sports or low-impact activities that tend to emphasize achievement of his/her personal best, perhaps combined with a love of the outdoors and an enthusiasm for life. This chapter presents ten creative projects for people who enjoy staying physically fit. Check off the projects that you might be interested in.

Projects in This Chapter: ✔

1. Join a Dance Group   ☐
2. Try T'ai Chi   ☐
3. Join a Fitness Club   ☐
4. Start a Walking Program   ☐
5. Indoor Walking for Apartment Dwellers   ☐
6. Get Fit with Strength Training   ☐
7. Try Aqua Fitness   ☐
8. Go on Nature Walks   ☐
9. Bicycle to Fitness   ☐
10. Try Tennis   ☐

Project One—Join a Dance Group

For the person who enjoys socializing, as well as keeping physically fit, joining a regular dance group can be fun. Three of the more popular types of dance groups for retirees are square dancing, line dancing, and ballroom dancing.

Square dancing still remains prevalent in most rural areas of North America and is practiced by regional square dancing associations that hold local dances for its members. Groups also travel to other districts either to compete in competitions or to celebrate with other square dancing enthusiasts. Dancing is done with a partner, in group formations of six to eight people. The music is usually provided by a live band and includes polkas, waltzes, and five or six specific square dance routines, sometimes aided by a freestyle *caller* who leads the dancers through spontaneous swirls and directional shifts during the dance. Participants usually include equal numbers of men and women between the ages of fifty and seventy-five. Competitions often involve specialized matching outfits, although local dance partners typically wear casual clothing. One variation on square dancing is called *clogging*, which involves tap shoes that match the beat of the music as you dance, reminiscent of Irish dancers.

Line dancing is a more recent phenomenon that has gained popularity through television dance shows. It's based entirely on country and western music and may be danced without a partner in a synchronized line formation (hence its name), or as couples with a partner. Typically, line dancing enthusiasts wear western outfits, blue jeans, cowboy boots, and black or white cowboy hats. The music may be provided by a disc jockey or a live band. Line dancing instruction is sometimes offered free on certain nights of the week at dance halls, and also as a fun exercise through night school hobby classes. Participants at dance halls often contain equal numbers of men and women between the ages of twenty-five and seventy-five.

Ballroom dancing is the most formal and graceful of the partnership dance styles and has existed for over 150 years. Students can take lessons through dance studios, church groups, and sometimes through night school hobby classes. The dress is very formal at the actual events, although not necessarily during the lessons. Men wear suits or tuxedos, and women wear beautiful swirling gowns puffed up with crinolines, and patent leather shoes. Opportunities for ballroom dancing occur at federal political functions, ballroom dance parties for young women who are "coming out," popular in the southern states, and New Year's Eve dances at the more expensive hotels. The music is provided by an orchestra often playing Big Band Era music from the thirties and forties, including composers such as George Gershwin, Glenn Miller, and Tommy Dorsey. Ballroom dance styles performed by the group may include the mambo, rhumba, tango, foxtrot, and waltz. Participants includes equal numbers of men and women between the ages of fifty and sixty-five. For additional information on these dance styles, refer to these resources available at video/DVD stores or from Amazon.com.

Square Dancing Today
by Christy Lane
VHS Tape
ASIN: 1889127434

This video will introduce you to the basic square dance calls and moves. Movements are shown step by step. Then the dances are performed to five different fiddle and high-energy techno songs.

Hot New Line Dances
Starring Christy Lane
VHS Tape
ASIN: 6302982863

Fast-paced line dancing video with good teaching techniques. You need to be in good shape for the hip hop sequences. Also Available: *More Hot New Line Dances.*

Ballroom Dancing
Starring Kyle and Susan Webb
VHS Tape
ASIN: 6305119430

Highly rated instructional video with repeated and slow motion dance steps, well suited to the beginning ballroom dancer. Also available: *Intermediate Level Ballroom Dancing.*

Project Two—Try T'ai Chi

T'ai Chi is a Chinese system of meditative and thera-
peutic exercises, which is characterized by methodi-
cally slow, circular, and stretching movements. The
words *T'ai* meaning peace, and *Chi* meaning breath,
energy, vitality, and force, give the meaning *peaceful
energy*. The discipline of T'ai Chi can produce both
physical and emotional well-being through the practice of breath control and slow concentrated moves. It
is of particular value for retirees who suffer symptoms
of stress, poor concentration, poor blood circulation,
muscular arthritis, or those who need to increase their
range of mobility.

T'ai Chi is also a martial art designed to increase breath
control and body balance while the body is in motion.
It is based on the notion of opposites, the Yin and the
Yang in nature. You are taught to wait for your opponent
to strike the first blow, then react to it. You avoid the
use of muscular or awkward force to block your
opponent. Instead, you rely on your inner energy and
the momentum of your opponent's force by changing
its direction in your favor, usually causing your
opponent to be off balance, or to fall with very little
effort. These martial art concepts can be seen within
the separate but equally graceful disciplines of Judo
and Kung Fu.

Advocates of this exercise regimen recommend it as
one of the finest ways to improve health, assist in
the circulation of blood, create tranquillity throughout the entire nervous system, and, through concentration, to create a deep peace of mind. Through the
harmony of mind and body comes great happiness

and good health. It's also a great way to wake up in the morning.

The best way to learn T'ai Chi is to take a course in it so that you can see the moves being demonstrated, practice proper breathing techniques, and receive advice and feedback from the instructor. Check the Y.M.C.A. or Y.W.C.A. for courses. A television or video demonstration can be moderately helpful. A book on T'ai Chi can explain the philosophy and illustrate the various positions, but it cannot adequately demonstrate the fluid movements of the participant. The following resources might be helpful.

The Complete Idiot's Guide to
T'ai Chi & Qi Gong
by Bill Douglas, and Richard Vennie
MacMillan, 1998
ISBN 0028629094

Easy-to-follow introductory guide to T'ai Chi. Photographs accompany each exercise. Special section for seniors.

T'ai Chi for Beginners:
10 Minutes to Health & Fitness
by Clare Hooten
Berkley Publishing Group, 1996
ISBN 0399522077

A user-friendly guide for beginners. It offers illustrated instruction of the first twenty movements of the Yang style T'ai Chi. Designed as a ten-minute work-out.

T'ai Chi for Older Adults
by Dr. Paul Lam
VHS Tape, 1998
ASIN 188553891X

Great video for beginners. It uses a lot of repetition and slow motion instruction. Also available: *T'ai Chi Anywhere.*

T'ai Chi—The 24 Forms
by Dr. Paul Lam
VHS Tape, 1999
ASIN 1583500197

An excellent two-hour instructional video of the standardized 24 forms of T'ai Chi. Good follow-up to his beginner's tape.

Project Three—Join a Fitness Club

One of the best investments that you can make for longevity is in your physical health. Unless your health is good, retirement will not be an enjoyable stretch of time. The notion of physical fitness can be defined using three criteria: body flexibility, cardiovascular fitness, and muscle tone.

Body flexibility refers to the ease with which you can reach down to pick up something off the floor, or the degree of rotation in your arm and shoulder sockets when performing some task, or being able to turn your head to see something beside you or people behind you. People who are overweight or have mild arthritis should seek floor-style or aquatic group exercises that concentrate on stretching, joint rotation, and increased muscle flexibility. Aquatics is a great way to start this type of group exercise because the water buoyancy makes you feel lighter, while simultaneously offering a challenge by providing slight resistance to body movements.

Cardiovascular fitness refers to how your heart and lungs are performing compared to their optimum capacity. If you are short of breath after two minutes of exercise, then your heart and lungs are vastly under performing their potential. The goal of cardiovascular exercises is to increase your ability to perform physical tasks for a sustained period of time, without feeling tired or out of breath. Exercises such as outdoor jogging, jumping jacks, stationary bike riding, treadmills, stair stepping, or stair climbing are designed to increase cardiovascular fitness by making your heart rate and breathing rate rise above the normal rate of an inactive person for an extended period.

Muscle tone refers to body strength. How much weight can your legs and arms carry without difficulty? Do your groceries seem increasingly heavy? Can you pick up the grandkids in your arms without difficulty? Fitness machines, such as the leg press, chest press, arm curl, and abdomen cruncher, are designed to increase your body strength, and, as a side benefit, also firm up your muscles so you will look less flabby.

There are three types of organizations that most retired people turn to for fitness workshops and access to fitness equipment and swimming pools: the Y.M.C.A. or Y.W.C.A., family fitness centers, and community centers for seniors.

The Y.M.C.A., a not-for-profit service provider, usually offers fitness workshops specially aimed at seniors for a modest cost. The goal of their workshops are increased body flexibility and improved cardiovascular condition with some improvement of muscle tone. Full-service Y.M.C.A. centers often have a swimming pool, a sauna, an indoor running track, and a cluster of fitness equipment arranged in a numbered series for a systematic workout of body muscles (arms, waist, thighs, lower back, etc.). Some centers have a two-minute soft bell sound to remind clients that it's time to rotate to the next fitness machine. Using that method, a retiree can rotate through fifteen separate fitness machines in thirty minutes. The lunch-hour business crowd loves that feature because it needs to work out, shower, and get back to work all within an hour.

Family fitness centers are independent profit-motivated service providers that offer access to new fitness equipment in a pleasant bright setting. Memberships usually cost more than the Y.M.C.A. Many sport-oriented fitness centers also have a squash court, sauna, and swimming pool and may offer aquatic exercise workshops for seniors.

Community centers for seniors provide services that vary from one organization to another. These centers are often staffed by volunteers and offer floor-style group fitness workshops designed specifically for the senior age group. These workshops concentrate on increased flexibility and cardiovascular improvements rather than increased muscle tone. Most of the newer retirement communities provide a swimming pool in addition to group workshop exercise rooms and a limited range of exercise machines.

Project Four—Start a Walking Program

One easy way of exercising is to begin a simple walking program. All you need is a comfortable pair of walking shoes. Walking provides several benefits including increased muscle tone in your legs and improved cardiovascular fitness in your heart and lungs. It also gets you out of the house on a daily basis and if the sun is shining, you get a nice psychological boast to brighten your day.

Here are some suggestions for establishing your own walking program. Find a thirty-minute period in the day when you are typically undistracted from chores, such as before breakfast or later in the morning. Set aside that same time each day for a walk. Begin with a short walk the first week, perhaps three to four blocks, then gradually add more distance each week until your outdoor excursion totals twenty or thirty minutes. The secret to improved fitness it to walk fast enough and far enough to cause both your breathing and heart rate to increase. You should find yourself slightly out of breath when you get back home.

To make the outing more enjoyable, seek out walking trails in your neighborhood. You may be fortunate enough to be near a walking path through a wooded area that contains squirrels and chipmunks and a variety of trees and bushes to add visual and auditory interest to the walk. Some cities have attractive walking trails near the waterfront for added interest. One retired gentleman was known to get up at six o'clock each morning, drive to a waterfront pathway, and walk along the shoreline while watching the sun rise and the ducks and seagulls bobbing in the water. Then on his return to the starting point, he stopped for his morning cup of coffee at a nearby restaurant where his car was parked. What a refreshing and positive way to begin the day!

To add motivation and companionship, seek out a walking partner to share your excursions. Having someone to chat with on the trails makes the effort a more pleasant experience. The other person also provides impetus to get going each day.

Urban dwellers without easy access to a nature path may find that a headset and cassette/CD player with a favorite uplifting tape is a great way to drown out the engines, traffic, and other noises of the neighborhood as they take their walks. For additional information, refer to the following sources.

Fitness Walking for Dummies
by Liz Neporent
Hungry Minds, Inc., 1999
ISBN   0764551922

Exercise physiologist Liz Neporent covers everything you need to know to make walking a habit. You learn walking techniques, how to set up a routine, adding variety, and staying motivated.

The Healthy Heart Walking Book
by the American Heart Association
Hungry Minds, Inc., 1995
ISBN   0028604474

This spiral-bound edition provides advice for getting started, building endurance, assessing your fitness level, and choosing proper shoes. Highly rated.

Project Five—Indoor Walking For Apartment Dwellers

Perhaps you get cabin fever in the winter months, particularly if you live in the northern climates. Many creative high-rise apartment dwellers have found that the buildings in which they live have comfortable, weatherproof, built-in walking trails—the buildings' hallways. Modern apartment buildings tend to have stairwells at each end of the building. This creates a continuous walking trail for the those of you who wants to keep reasonably fit. Take the elevator to the top floor and walk the top hallway to the farthest stairwell, then descend to the next floor. On that floor, walk the complete hallway to the opposite stairwell, descend one flight, and begin the process once again. When you get tired, take the elevator back to your own floor. A typical twelve-story building may have as much as a quarter to a half mile of walkways.

Apartment buildings also have definite quiet times during the day when there are few people around. Choose a time when you can walk without distraction, such as early in the morning before most renters have left for work, or after nine o'clock when they have already gone. Other quiet periods usually occur after lunch and in the evenings.

You may wish to experiment with different walking clothes. Some people prefer to wear a track suit and running shoes to put them in the proper frame of mind, while other people just go in regular clothes. Some hallway walkers also use a pedometer to measure the walking distance they have covered in miles or kilometers to keep track of their progress.

For a more difficult workout, reverse the walking process by beginning on the bottom floor and taking the stairway up to each successive floor before walking the length of that floor. This adds the burden of lifting your body weight up a flight of stairs before each walk, increasing your heart rate and breathing rate considerably.

If you are very athletic, try walking up the entire stairwell from the bottom floor to the top of the building each day. Work your way up gradually. Try walking halfway for a week, then each successive week add one additional floor until you can master the whole stairwell in one attempt. Be forewarned, though, this is extremely taxing on your heart and lungs and will leave you breathing heavily for several minutes after the workout. Indeed, on your first attempt, you may take half an hour to recover. If done in gradual increments, though, stair climbing can be a successful way to increase lower body muscular strength, expand cardiovascular capabilities, and diminish recovery time to as little as ten minutes. Not recommended for those with untreated high blood pressure or heart ailments.

Project Six—Get Fit With Strength Training

If you watch other seniors working out in gyms and health centers, you may notice that most of them will automatically gravitate toward the treadmills and cycling endurance machines. Most seniors mistakenly believe that these machines offer the only way lose weight and to slenderize their bodies.

In the book *Strength Training Past Fifty*, authors Westcott and Baechle describe the surprising results of their five-year study. The participants worked out on twelve resistance strength training machines for thirty minutes three times a week. They discovered that former couch potatoes, both men and women in the sixty-one to eighty age category, responded as well to strength training as did the younger groups. Although all participants made impressive improvements, those starting in the less fit categories added the most muscle, lost the most fat, and experienced the greatest reduction in resting blood pressure. In other words, those who needed strength training exercises the most benefited the most. After working with seniors as old as eighty-four, the researchers concluded that there is simply no age limit on strength training and muscle building.

Strength training with exercise machines showed improvements in several areas: added muscle tissue, increased metabolic rate, reduced body fat, increased bone density, improved glucose levels, faster digestive processes, lower blood pressure, improved cholesterol levels, reduced back pain, and reduced arthritic pain.

Dieters, in particular, will find this program a useful way to break out of the yo-yo cycle of weight loss and weight gain. It may sound silly at first, but the problem with calorie-reduced diets is that the dieter loses an equal amount of fat and muscle tissue. So not only does the calorie-reduced dieter become physically weaker, but he/she also suffers a reduction in the body's ability to burn fat in the future.

Due to muscle loss, adults lose about 5 percent of their fat-burning metabolism each decade. Every pound of muscle uses dozens of calories a day just to sustain itself. So when you lose muscle, the calories that were previously used to maintain muscle tissue now go directly into fat storage. By increasing muscle tissue through the use of strength training machines, participants increase their fat-burning engines and became slimmer. And it works for people of any age.

The next time you are in a fitness center, ask a training consultant to teach you how to use the various resistance machines and make them part of your thirty-minute workout. As with all exercise, use a gradual approach. Use light weights for resistance and increase the weight levels gradually over several weeks as your strength improves. For additional information, readers should refer to the following resources.

Weight Training for Dummies
by Liz Neporent, and Suzanne Schlosberg
Hungry Minds, Inc., 2000
ISBN 076455168X

This guide is written by two knowledgeable and per-sonal fitness trainers. They also co-authored *Fitness for Dummies.*

Strength Training Past Fifty
by Wayne L. Westcott, Ph.D.
and Thomas R. Baechle, Ed.D.
Human Kinetics, 1998
ISBN 0-88011-716-8

Describes the results of a 5-year strength-training study and provides illustrations of the various machines used by the participants. Great technical background for fitness instructors working with seniors.

Project Seven—Try Aqua Fitness

Aqua Fitness refers to exercise routines done in a pool, something that is rising in popularity among seniors. Offered by the Y.M.C.A., health spas, and fitness clubs, aqua fitness involves doing exercises while standing chest deep in a pool. The water provides resistant to movement of your arms and legs while the fitness instructor leads you through various stretching and strength training routines in thirty-minute to forty-five minute sessions.

This approach to fitness is preferable for older participants who have decreased bone density and muscle mass (which the water exercises help to rebuild) over the traditional high-impact, endurance-building, calorie-reducing floor exercises designed specifically for younger participants in their twenties and thirties. Aqua fitness concentrates on improving flexibility of movement and achieving moderate improvements in strength and endurance.

Those of you who attend aqua fitness three times a week should see noticeable improvement in body flexibility within a few weeks. Long-term improvements in cardiovascular rates (heart and breathing), lower cholesterol, and lower blood pressure will begin within three to six months along with an improved self-image and general feeling of well being. Light to moderate weight loss will occur over the long term as muscle mass increases.

If you are arthritic, overweight, have back or leg problems, tender tootsies, problems with head or neck rotation, or difficulty raising your arms above your shoulders, you may benefit significantly from this type of exercise. These conditions, which usually make traditional high-impact training or strength-training machines unsuitable, present less difficulty in warm pool water where your body becomes buoyant and the water provides a slight resistance to movement. It is a great starting point for those of you who have been longtime professional couch potatoes.

Project Eight—Go On Nature Walks

Most towns and cities have nature walking trails for you to stroll outdoors in the fresh air while getting the fitness exercise provided by the walking. The advantage of taking nature strolls rather than walks along city streets is the positive psychological effect that trees, flowers, singing birds, busy squirrels, blue skies, and fresh air have on you. Trees also act as a natural air filter, taking in carbon dioxide and letting out oxygen as part of their growing process. A tree-lined pathway is inherently more healthy and refreshing than a city sidewalk situated near passing cars emitting toxic clouds of carbon dioxide, carbon monoxide, and carbon particles. Trees also give off their own unique fresh natural smell.

Look for nature walks in city parks, along ravines and river banks, and near lake and ocean fronts. A walk along a sandy beach with waves gently washing ashore is a great place to find tiny seashells or interesting pieces of wood suitable for carving. Some cities have developed interesting bike paths that wind along wooded areas or former railway tracks. These city trails are often shared by cyclists, roller skate enthusiasts, walkers, and joggers. Areas with lakes or ocean vistas usually have paved waterfront walking trails with picturesque scenery full of sailboats, seagulls, pelicans, people fishing off the piers, and gorgeous sunrises and sunsets.

If you intend to become a nature enthusiast, come prepared for your outings with a comfortable pair of running shoes, a jogging outfit, a camera if scenery is spectacular, and a small bottle of water tucked away in a waist belt. Some nature walkers become tree experts, developing an expertise in tree identification, or combine walking with the hobby of bird watching and become proficient at identifying various types of birds in the area with the help of a pocket field guide. Residents of large urban centers are often surprised to find that there are several nature walking and hiking trails within city limits or within an hours drive of the city. There are nature trail books written for almost all major North American urban centers and some for entire states. For example, within the five boroughs of New York, there are more than twenty-six thousand acres of parkland, and within a ninety-minute radius of Times Square there are thirteen hundred miles of walking/hiking trails. Whether you live in a particular area or are traveling by car on vacation and need a refreshing outdoor break, do some research and find the locations of the local walking trails. Check the health-fitness section of a local bookstore for information.

This is too beautiful a continent to spend all of our lives indoors. When the weather is suitable, athletes should seek out the nature trails. The air is healthier, the scenery is more enjoyable, and the sunshine will be a guaranteed morale booster.

For additional information, readers should refer to the following sources. These represent just a sampling of available walking/hiking books:

Nature Walks in and Around New York City
by Sheila Buff
Appalachian Mountain Club, 1996
ISBN 1878239538

Twelve of the walks are in New York City proper and the rest are in the surrounding counties and states. All sites feature wildlife, birds, and plants and are very scenic.

Nature Walks in New Jersey
by Glenn Scherer
Appalachian Mountain Club, 1998
ISBN 1878239686

This guide covers the best trails from the highlands to Cape May and describes 46 nature walks. With an average length of 4 miles, these trails are well-suited to the seasoned hiker.

75 Year-Round Hikes in Northern California
by Marc J. Soares
Mountaineer's Books, 2000
ISBN 0898867207

An all-season hikers guide to trails in Northern California. A useful appendix cross references trails by views, waterfalls, redwoods, and wildlife.

Nature Walks in and Around Seattle
by Cathy McDonald, and Stephen Whitney
Mountaineer's Books, 1997, 2nd Edition
ISBN 0898865255

Terrific guide to Seattle area parks. It has maps of trails and lists hours of operation, park features, steep steep trails, picnic facilities, and parking areas.

Project Nine—Bicycle To Fitness

Fortunately for retirees, most communities across the country have developed recreational bike/hiking paths to encourage outdoor activities. These facilities include park trails, intra-city bike pathways, former railway track-line trails, and river or lakefront trails. Exercising outdoors in the fresh air and sunshine is an invigorating and healthy pastime for those of us who wish to sail through our golden years with low risks of heart disease or osteoporosis. These are reasons why recreational biking has become a popular outdoor activity among seniors.

Sporting goods stores offer a confusing range of bikes for sale. They sell mountain bikes with thick treads, which are designed for rough, off-road terrain. Slim racing bikes with their bull-horn handle bars and tiny seats are designed for competitive cross-country racing. The best categories for those interested in short bike rides at a comfortable pace are the hybrids—bikes that allow the rider to sit upright and have lots of small gears, some as many as twenty-four gears, to make peddling easier. The bike cruisers, for example, look like an old traditional Schwinn-model bike with balloon tires and are well-suited for riding on pavement or level bike paths.

Biking attire has changed somewhat over the years. Biking helmets are legal requirements in some jurisdictions and a sound investment for all biking enthusiasts. Water bottles that attach to the bike frame are a good idea on hot summer days, as are polarizing sunglasses that remove the sun's glare on the asphalt. Optional accessories, including leather riding gloves and elbow pads, are great safety features for preventing scratches and abrasions on your hands and arms if you and the bike happen to tip over for some reason.

You may prefer the early morning or early evening as your biking activity time because traffic is minimal and the sun's rays are less harsh on the skin. Midday sun can be very hot and tends to sap your energy unless the trail is partly shaded. Trails that offer both trees for shade and bench seats on which to relax are highly recommended.

If you are on a long car trip you might consider bringing your bikes along with you to get a bit of exercise during your stay overs in various towns and parks. Or better still, research locations where bike rentals and biking trails are easily available before the trip begins and include them in your cross-country jaunt.

There are a number of organizations that offer active lifestyle vacations for seniors. These outdoor holidays, which may include hiking, walking, or biking, can be found in the United States, Canada, England, and Europe. Elderhostel catalogs have biking excursions in Virginia and Arizona as well as international locations. (In their catalog, look under the back section titled "Active Outdoor.") A company called Active Journeys offers bike-riding vacations in the English, Irish, and Scottish countrysides, through the Black Forest area in Germany and sleepy villages in Spain, and an Austrian bike trail near the Danube River.

There are two types of bike tours. The first are escorted tours in which a guide who knows the area and the local language travels with the group of bikers and offers historical titbits along the journey. The other is an unescorted tour in which adventurous travelers get their bikes, helmets, and a map from the travel agent and set off on their own across the countryside. In some tour packages, the hotels and restaurants are pre-booked and are typically located fifty miles apart from each other. The assumption in either case is that you are already active bike riders and are physically fit. For active vacations that include cross-country biking, contact the following organizations for their latest catalogs.

Elderhostel, Inc.
11 Avenue de Lafayette
Boston, Massachusetts
02111-1746
Website: www.elderhostel.org

Elderhostel provides several outdoor programs that involve walking, hiking, and bicycling, both in North America and in Europe.

Active Journeys
4891 Dundas Street W
Toronto, Ontario
Canada M9A 1B2
Telephone: 416-236-5011
Website: www.activejourneys.com

This tour agency offers escorted tours for seniors in the United States, Canada, Britain, and Switzerland. All involve walking, hiking, or bicycling. Ask for their brochure.

Project Ten—Try Tennis

Individuals who have maintained an active lifestyle prior to retirement might consider trying tennis as a recreational outlet. It's a more physically demanding sport than golf, but it can be played year round and those who pursue it on a regular basis tend to remain fit well into old age. The game can be played as singles (one person playing against one other person) or doubles with two people on each side.

If you are a beginner, it is recommended that you take ten to twelve lessons from a tennis instructor who will illustrate proper techniques, strategies, and how to score the game. There are inexpensive public tennis courts, which are usually outdoors and played on an asphalt surface. Some courts that belong to apartment buildings are free, but most are owned by local tennis clubs and require a $10/hour user fee. This can be split between the players. Busy tennis courts require that you book time on the court well in advance.

Private tennis clubs offer multiple indoor courts with a clay or rubberized surface, change rooms, and sometimes a refreshment bar. Court fees range from $25-$30/hour in prime time (8 A.M. to 6 P.M.) and $10/hour in nonprime time. In addition, tennis clubs may require an annual membership fee. The more exclusive the club, the higher the fee, which can reach as high as $1,200 to $1,500 a year.

There are other costs related to playing tennis, including the purchase of proper tennis shoes and a white tennis outfit. Tennis rackets can range in price from $50 to $300 and may be made out of titanium or carbon fibre. Oversized rackets permit a bigger sweep and are recommended for older players. It is also recommended that you join a national tennis association, which ranks your level of play and then matches players in your region who have the same level of expertise. Women have their own tennis association and their own set of rules.

Tennis provides both an athletic and social environment for the players. Various tournaments are played during the year, including a Seniors' Tournament. Ages are grouped in ten-year increments, such as fifty-one to sixty, sixty-one to seventy, and so on. There are tennis players in their seventies and early eighties who still enjoy four moderately paced games three times a week. It is an active fitness sport that promotes body flexibility, cardiovascular fitness, and arm and leg muscle toning. Those are worthwhile goals for those of you who wish to remain active. For additional references, you may wish to refer to the following resources.

Tennis for Dummies
by McEnroe, Fink, and Bodo
Hungry Minds, Inc., 1998
ISBN 07645508X

Practical advice with a humorous touch. Provides tips, tactics, and techniques for beginning to intermediate players.

The Inner Game of Tennis
by W. Timothy Gallwey
Random House, 1997
ISBN 0679778314

Billie Jean King once called this book her "tennis bible." This second edition has theories on concentration, gamesmanship, trusting yourself, and breaking bad habits. Also available on audiocassette.

Tennis Our Way
by Arthur Ashe, Stan Smith, and Vic Braden
ASIN 6300279855 VHS

A coaching video from three tennis legends. It covers tennis from the basics to the advanced. Includes slow motion sequences. Video. 2½ hours.

Chapter Fourteen

Projects For Deferred Retirement

Not all retirees want to stop working. The motivations may be financial, emotional, or just the sheer boredom with the extensive unscheduled time that retirement brings into one's life. Many retirees, who feel physically fit and like the routine and discipline that a regular job brings, will seek out a full- or part-time job. The job may be a second career or something completely different from what they used to do. This chapter presents ten interesting jobs that as a retiree, you might consider. Check off the projects that you might be interested in.

Projects in This Chapter: ✔

1. Start a New Career ☐
2. Become a Travel Escort ☐
3. Be a Car Rental Agency Shuttle Driver ☐
4. Sell Your Caregiver Talents ☐
5. Become a Professional House Sitter ☐
6. Research Family Trees for a Fee ☐
7. Refinish and Sell Antique Furniture ☐
8. Deliver for a Pharmacy ☐
9. Organize a Musical Group ☐
10. Teach Golf or Tennis to Beginners ☐

Creative Retirement

Project One—Start a New Career

For many successful independent-thinking people, the fun of working was in the process of striving to achieve their initial career goals—to become the head of marketing or the company president, for example. Maybe the goal was to earn a million dollars before the age of fifty or become known as a master craftsman or one of the best experts in a chosen field. Striving to attain a goal, despite the hardships and challenges, can make life interesting, exciting, and personally rewarding.

For most people, those challenges disappear when they retire. If you are one of those people who still needs that challenge to make life interesting and give you a reason for jumping out of bed in the morning, consider starting a second career. After twenty or thirty years in a profession or trade, you have become extremely good at a number of tasks and skills that can be applied to a new career.

One army sergeant, for example, spent his military career working with sophisticated target acquisitioning systems in tanks and armored vehicles. When forced into mandatory retirement at the age of fifty, he began a new career working as a field consultant for a company that manufactured and marketed weapon targeting systems. He traveled to various army bases as a consultant, checking the accuracy of newly installed weapon systems.

Retirees who formerly managed office complexes, manufacturing plants, or data processing departments or nurtured a start up business into a successful enterprise also make great business consultants. Small fledgling businesses that sell products and services often get into trouble as they grow larger and need outside expertise to provide advice and direction.

No matter what your past career has been, you still have an array of skills that can be put to use in another direction. Make a list of the skills that you have developed over the years, such as people management, problem-solving, crisis intervention and resolution, creative development, marketing, teaching, technical, computers, writing, or artistic design. Then, make a list of possible careers that can use those talents.

Retirees can become mentors, teachers, consultants, new business developers, service providers, legal advisors, investors, tradespeople, truck drivers, photographers, freelance authors, interior decorators, political advisors, and senior travel consultants. There really is no limit to what you can do if your heart is set on it. Feeling like there is a purpose and direction to your life may be the key to a happier semi-retirement. For additional information for those contemplating a second career, refer to the following resources.

The Complete Idiot's Guide to
Starting a Home-Based Business
by Barbara Weltman, and Beverly Williams
Alpha Books, 2000, 2nd Edition
ISBN 0028638425

Highly rated book on the ins and outs of owning a home business. Covers types of businesses, financing, taxation, marketing, the home office, and keeping your personal and business lives separate. A primer for success.

Turn Your Passion Into Profits:
How to Start the Business of Your Dreams
by Janet Allon
Hearst Books, 2001
ISBN   1588160068

Equal parts information and inspiration, this book will teach you what you need to know about starting the business of your dreams. A *New York Times* writer, Allon uses actual case studies from women entrepreneurs. Topics: business plans, business name, financing, marketing, and hiring staff.

Project Two—Become a Travel Escort

All-inclusive packaged tours to various domestic and exotic destinations, such as Britain, Europe, Australia, Russia, and China, have become increasingly popular methods of travel with this generation of retirees. Many people love to travel, but many prefer that someone else plan the details of the itinerary and do the organizing. Escorted tours fill this niche in the travel industry. These extended trips may involve several methods of transportation, including planes, tour buses, passenger trains, or cruise ships. Passengers travel together as a group accompanied by a representative of the travel agency referred to as a travel escort.

The travel escort is part guide, part entertainer, part organizer, and part troubleshooter. This is also the person who handles the day-to-day details of the trip, such as room assignments for sleeping, making sure the luggage gets to the rooms, getting people up at 6:00 A.M. for breakfast and onto the rest of the tour. He or she may also provide a travelogue over the audio system of interesting things to see and has daily chats with each person in the group.

Not surprisingly, agencies that hire travel escorts tend to favor escorts who love being with people, over people who just love to travel. Frequent travelers will often request trips on which their favorite travel escort is working.

Veteran travel escorts will learn the names of the group

members before the tour begins and send them welcome letters a week ahead of time, with travel tips on which items to bring, as well as health insurance suggestions. They often have a set of personal audio cassettes with six to eight hours of pleasant travel music, a jug of water and disposable cups (and garbage bag) for passengers, a bag of toffees and candies, a first aid kit, puzzles, brain teasers and pencils, and anecdotes to entertain passengers on monotonous long stretches of travel.

Escort pay is meager and varies by the agency. It may range from $350 to $500 (plus tips) for a three-week tour, or they may be paid $80 to $150 per day depending on their experience and ability. Agencies will often placate their best escorts by offering them their favorite travel venues instead of more money. Most escorts, however, enjoy the adventure of meeting a new group of people and the thrill of travel. The experience is like a box of chocolates: you never know what you are going to get until you bite into them.

Project Three—Be A Car Rental Agency Shuttle Driver

Car rental agencies, such as Avis and Tilden, advertise in retirement newspapers and magazines specifically for retirees to serve as shuttle drivers for their fleet of cars. The problem for which they need your help is that customers often drop off a rental car in a location other than its point of origin. Since rental agencies are independently owned, and that car is the owners' corporate property, they need to get it back to their rental agency lot as soon as possible. So they charge the customer an additional drop-off fee of $20 to $50, depending on the distance, and use that money to pay their team of shuttle drivers. The larger the agency and the bigger the urban center, the greater number of trips the shuttle driver can expect per day.

Shuttle drivers may work within a single metropolitan center shuttling cars between different agency locations, airports and inner city locations, different cities, or frequented cross-border routes. Usually retirees are offered the local shuttle jobs.

Typically, car rental agencies look for enthusiastic retirees with a valid driver's "G class" (general) license or better, free of traffic violations, who are available on call with flexible hours to drive their vehicles. Interested candidates will be required to present their driver's license, which may be photocopied and kept on file, and a short one-page resume with their name, mailing address, phone number, and social security or insurance number. It may be helpful to have a cell phone or pager so that the company can keep tabs on you while you're in transit or waiting for a new assignment.

To apply for these jobs, seek out local independently owned car rental agencies and ask the rental manager about job availabilities and a possible job interview at which you can drop off your resume for their files. The larger the agency, the greater the need. Look for franchises that have a national brand car rental name, such as Avis, Tilden, National, and Budget. You can find them in your telephone book's yellow pages.

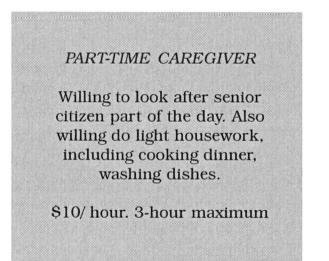

PART-TIME CAREGIVER

Willing to look after senior citizen part of the day. Also willing do light housework, including cooking dinner, washing dishes.

$10/ hour. 3-hour maximum

Project Four—Sell Your Caregiver Talents

If you enjoy taking care of other people, but also have need of part-time income, you might consider selling your caregiving skills by the hour. With the increased number of elderly people in North American cities and towns, the need for caregivers has also increased. People need someone to assist with elderly parents or individuals with debilitating arthritis, loss of memory, or a recent injury, or some lonesome relative who just needs a little company while younger relatives are out shopping or need a break from being the full-time caregiver.

Advertise as a part-time caregiver for $10 to $20 per hour, depending on the difficulty and complexity of the assignment. If an assignment sounds too difficult, refuse to take it. Schedule your assignments so that you also have free time for yourself. Relieving full-time caregivers for a couple hours each week can be scheduled on particular days well in advance so that both of you can make other plans.

Some substitute caregivers offer a range of skills, including cooking lunch or supper, washing dishes, light housekeeping, chatting with an infirm patient, or reading newspapers or books to someone who is losing his/her eyesight.

In large apartment buildings, you can advertise your skills on the laundry room bulletin board or on their social activity board. Include your hourly rate, what tasks you are willing to do, and tear-away strips with your phone number. Other inexpensive locations where you can advertise include neighborhood grocery store bulletin boards, the Internet, a local seniors' newspaper, and at senior community centers. You may wish to advertise in the classified section of a local newspaper for about $15 a week under the section Caregiving Help Offered. Specify the distance you are willing to travel. Sample advertisements are shown below.

Project Five—Become a Professional House Sitter

One interesting nonstrenuous part-time paying job for singles or couples that involves travel to different parts of the country is house sitting. At any point in time, a certain number of homeowners all over North America are planning extensive vacations, temporary career relocations, or lengthy hospital recuperation that cause them to be absent from their homes for a certain length of time. They may be worried that during their absence their home will be broken into or vandalized, or that their flower garden and lawn will die from neglect. The solution to their problem is to find a responsible individual or retired married couple who will act as caretakers for their property while they are gone.

If homeowners cannot convince a relative or neighbor to take the assignment, they will often resort to advertising in a national newspaper, a retirement or seniors magazine, the classified section in a senior association website, or through house sitting agencies. The advertisements will specify the region of the country where the house is located and the length of time that the homeowner will be absent. Since the house sitting assignment involves a vacation of sorts for the house sitter in a different climate, it is considered as part of the pay. The rest of your salary is negotiated with the homeowner who may also be willing to pay for some of your travel costs.

If you are considering such a vacation/assignment, you should develop a one-page resume, complete with a current photograph, name, address, phone number, age, past careers, and short biography. Homeowners seeking house sitting candidates tend to prefer nonsmoking retired couples with past careers that indicate stability and responsibility, such as retired police officers or security officers, teachers, doctors, ministers, or store owners. They also look for people who will not stray far from the house, such as writers or painters who are looking for privacy and a quiet retreat.

You can find advertisements for house sitting in retirement magazines, such as *Fifty-Plus* and *Good Times,* both published in Toronto, Canada. The *Caretaker Gazette* is a bimonthly newsletter published in Arizona, devoted to 700 house sitting, property, and caretaking opportunities. For additional information, refer to the following sources.

The Caretaker Gazette
PO Box 5887-M
Carefree, Arizona
85377-1970
Phone: 480-488-1970
Website: www.caretaker@uswest.net

This bimonthly newsletter outlines 700 house sitting, property, and caretaking opportunities. Subscription cost $27/year. AskforGary Dunn.

There are dozens of regional housesitting agencies in the United States and Canada. To access them try the following Internet Keywords: house sitting agencies

AARP (American Association of Retired Persons)
Website : www.aarp.org
For house sitting opportunities, check out the AARP website classified ads.

Fifty-Plus (Canadian Association of Retired Persons)
Website: www.fifty-plus.net
Telephone: 416-363-5562

Each bimonthly issue of CARP's magazine for seniors has classified ads requesting house sitters, frequently on the Pacific coast.

Good Times
E-mail: goodtimes@mail.transcontinental.ca
Fax: 1-416-340–8000
Telephone: 1-800–465-8443
Their bimonthly magazine for seniors contains classified ads requesting house sitters.

Project Six—Research Family Trees For a Fee

Genealogy, the researching of one's family ancestry, has become a popular hobby among seniors in the past thirty years. However, many hobbyists are unable to do archival or graveyard headstone research on their own in a particular area of the country because of great distances or personal physical disabilities. As a result, they hire someone in the region where they suspect their ancestors lived to do the research for them.

Being a family history researcher can be a source of income if you charge clients a consulting fee for services provided. The fee can be by the hour or a flat fee for each task performed. For example, suppose a client has asked for census, marriage, death, and headstone information on a particular relative who was born in the 1800s. The census, marriage, and death data can be researched on microfilm in a state archive (or the National Archives if you live near Washington) or in a Family History Center of the Latter Day Saints. The headstone information can be obtained from an actual visit to the cemetery, reading through headstone transcription records found in printed cemetery records, or on some cemetery Internet websites. The client can be charged $10 to $20 per hour based on time spent on the tasks, or by a varying flat fees, such as $10 for a census or marriage record on one individual, $5 for each headstone transcription, and $10 for headstone photographs. The fees are always collected before the research begins.

The job itself requires knowledge about where information can be found, patience, a willingness to help people, and skills in operating your own business. You will need a suitable filing system to keep track of multiple clients, and a computer system to do research, write letters, and print invoice details of services rendered. Designing letterhead stationery for invoices and letters will provide a professional appearance to your work. If you dedicate the computer, filing cabinet and furniture, supplies, and Internet fees entirely to the business, you can claim an office in the home and use them as legitimate tax deductions against revenue earned from the business.

Marketing your services is going to be one of the on going operational costs. Some suggestions include developing a business website, printing professional brochures, designing a business logo, and advertising in family history journals and genealogy society newsletters in distant locations, such as other states or other countries (Canada or Britain).

You may find that specializing as an expert in one particular region, one ethnic group, or the Civil War era will draw more clients than advertising as a general researcher. Base your advertising on things you are already familiar with and have already researched.

Creative Retirement

Project Seven—Refinish and Sell Antique Furniture

Retirees who are good with their hands and enjoy working with wood-related projects should consider purchasing, refinishing, and selling antique furniture as an income-generating venture. The furniture pieces might include old hutches, end tables, dresser drawers, wash stands, bookcases, rocking chairs, kitchen chairs, and tables. There are a number of places where early manufactured furniture can be obtained, including summer garage sales, particularly in small towns with old houses and in farm country; home foreclosures auctions; estate sales; and from friends, relatives, and neighbors.

The main refinishing tools are those designed to strip away old paint and varnish, such as belt sanders for smooth surfaces and the Black & Decker Mouse for getting in and around odd shapes. All the hardware should be taken off the furniture prior to stripping, including brass or wooden knobs, openers, and latches.

Once the refinishing is completed, look for imperfections in the furniture—dents, scrapes, wood bubbles—and smooth those out as much as possible. Then apply some plastic wood to fill in the holes and imperfections and let dry.

How the surface covering is reapplied depends upon the type of furniture. Hutches, end tables, and book-cases will look rich in a dark mahogany varnish, while some pioneer dresser drawers and kitchen tables may look better with a sealant and clear coating for a rustic, unfinished appearance.

Once the hardware is reattached, the completed project is ready for resale. Pricing and selling the pieces is a business skill as important as the woodworking itself. The prices must not exceed what a new piece of furniture would cost, but should be enough to cover the cost of its original purchase plus a 15 to 20 percent profit. Presentation and display of the items is important to getting your asking price. Move the furniture out of the garage or workshop into an attractive setting and add doilies and vases of attractive plastic or real flowers to accent the furniture. Place small nicely lettered price tags on the pieces you are selling.

Another variation on this type of project is to start a business in which you refinish damaged wood furniture for clients. Usually more knowledge is required for this type of venture, including how to use wood laminates, match existing shades of varnish and stains, and use woodworking machines to make exact copies of damaged furniture parts.

Project Eight—Deliver For a Pharmacy

There are all sorts of product delivery positions open for seniors, including pizza delivery, restaurant delivery, and pharmacy delivery. However, they differ in several respects. Pizza and restaurant delivery positions are usually night shift jobs that begin at 4 P.M. and end at 1 A.M. or 2 A.M. As anyone that has done shift work can attest, night shifts will alter your lifestyle, sleeping patterns, and reduce daytime friendships. Usually the food industry requires that you provide and maintain your own vehicle, including gasoline, insurance, depreciation, and possible vehicle theft while making a night delivery. The rate of pay is usually minimum wage or a flat rate of pay, such as $1.25 for each completed delivery, plus any tips from the customers.

Pharmacy delivery is a daytime job with regular hours, typically from 10 A.M. to 5 P.M. Drug stores usually provide a car or pickup truck with their logo on it for you to make deliveries. The store is responsible for paying for the gasoline and maintenance of the vehicle. Most of your clients will be elderly and in dire need of the products you bring. Your rate of pay is minimum wage plus infrequent tips from sickly but thankful customers.

You will most likely make less money working for a pharmacy, than for a fast food provider because the tips and number of trips are fewer. On the other hand, the hours are more suited to seniors, the vehicle and accident liability are the store's responsibility, and the social status as a pharmacy driver is much superior to the others and is often perceived just short of an ambulance driver in importance.

To seek a position as a pharmacy driver, consider the smaller independent pharmacies that provide home deliveries rather than the major pharmacies located in shopping malls that depend on walk-in customers for their business. Refer to the yellow pages of your telephone directory to find those stores that offer home delivery. A second source of job openings may appear in the want ads of your local newspaper. Be prepared to begin as a part-time driver, and bring a friendly smile and positive attitude to the job interview.

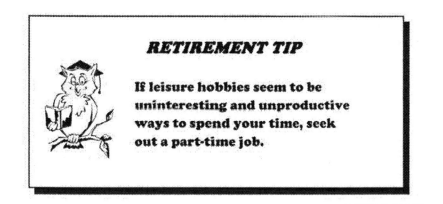

RETIREMENT TIP

If leisure hobbies seem to be uninteresting and unproductive ways to spend your time, seek out a part-time job.

Project Nine—Organize a Musical Group

Retirees who are musically talented might consider organizing a musical group for pleasure and/or profit. The group might specialize in specific ethnic music, such as polkas or Irish music. It could be a Scottish marching pipe band. It may be a classical ensemble of strings and brass that plays at concerts and benefits, or it might be a traditional guitar band that plays pop or country music at traditional dances, square dances, and fall fairs. The group may concentrate on instrumental music or have a lead singer or a group of singers whose voices harmonize with the instruments.

The group needs a place to practice where they won't disturb the neighbors. This might a rented hall, someone's basement, an empty barn, a Legion Hall on non-event days, or a senior community center. The group may consider trading free performances at a dance hall in return for permission to practice there in the early mornings or when the place is normally empty.

Someone from within the group or from outside the group acts as the business manager. That person becomes responsible for booking performances, arranging for payment, and paying each of the performers. That person may also arrange for advertising, transportation, and accommodation for out-of-town performances. It helps if someone in the group owns a large van for transporting the musical instruments as well as the players.

If you are into this, members should decide how much time they wish to spend giving performances and being away from home. Do you wish to be performing both Friday and Saturday nights in addition to attending practices during the week? Do you agree to performing at out-of-town venues? Knowing the limits of your participation will reduce potential friction as the band gains in popularity and success. It will also make the business manager's job easier in selecting and arranging for performances. Successful groups may perform at banquet hall weddings, golf club dances, conventions, senior centers, church halls, outdoor concerts at fall fairs, and pubs, and earn a steady income. Just because you are retired doesn't mean that your target listening audience has to be of the same age group. All types of organizations are willing to pay for good musical groups who provide top entertainment, regardless of their age.

Project Ten—Teach Golf or Tennis to Beginners

Golf and tennis are two outdoor activities that usually require some initial training to master. The easiest way to learn the fundamentals of these games is to have someone coach you. If you are reasonably good at either game and you have the patience to work with beginners, you should consider offering your services as a personal instructor for retirees.

As a personal instructor for people in your own age group, you will satisfy several personal needs, including socializing, being outdoors in the fresh air, exercise, and earning money while you are doing it. You might consider offering introductory package deals with fixed prices for the beginner. For example: three-day workshops for $45, five-day workshops for $75, and ten-day workshops for $115. Offer a discount for husband and wife teams who wish to learn the sport together in combined one-hour sessions. Collect the fees prior to beginning the series of workshops. Also explain to clients the costs of tennis court fees or golf green fees in addition to their instruction fee and why the organizations charge them. A free initial meeting with clients should be arranged to collect the coaching fee, explain equipment and apparel requirements, and tell them what they will learn in the series of workshops, learn the dates of the workshops, answer their questions, and teach the basic grip and some simple techniques of the golf or tennis swing. You might consider the use of a van or four-wheel drive to transport your clients with their equipment to various training locations. Always go to those training locations several days beforehand and talk to the manager about what you are doing and when. Check for available times and extra costs. If you attract several clients at the same time, schedule them on alternate days rather than sequentially, to keep their interest in attending. That is one group meets Monday, Wednesday, and Friday, and the other group meets Sunday, Tuesday, and Thursday.

Golf is the more popular of the two activities and will draw more potential clients. The golf workshops may include sessions at a driving range, a putting range, and 9 or 18-hole games for the graduates. Public golf courses will be cheaper and more accessible, unless you have arranged discounts and permission from a private golf course to teach students on their property. The actual game will need four players including yourself whereas the training sessions on the driving or putting ranges will not. Past graduates may be happy to make up a third and fourth when needed. Keep their phone numbers for such an occasion, if they are interested.

Tennis is by far the more athletic of the two sports and general fitness is a consideration in selecting clients, particularly among the retirees. Be sure to book court time in advance, and explain your needs to management for having twosome and threesome workshops. Public tennis courts are less expensive than private tennis clubs, unless you have a membership and guest privileges.

Marketing your services is critical to a successful coaching venture, along with word-of-mouth advertising. It is recommended that you design and print a color fold-out brochure (using PrintMaster software or professional printers) that contains a front graphic of someone playing the sport, title, description of the course, workshop packages and their costs, and instructor's name and phone number. A professional-looking business card with a suitable sports graphic along with your name, title (Personal Golf Instructor), phone number, and e-mail address is a great method of advertising and small enough to pass out to friends and neighbors to drum up business.

Suggested locations for advertising include senior center bulletin boards and monthly newsletters, personal guest appearances at senior centers to explain what services you are offering, retirement planning conventions (lots of potential business clients), and the classified section of the newspaper. Other locations include apartment activity bulletin boards and grocery store community bulletin boards. Female coaches might consider having "women-only" workshops to attract a growing female market segment and to make their clients comfortable. Your biggest advertisement will always be your smile and personal charm with clients. Aim to be a coach who is fun and enjoyable to be with, and clients will line up to take classes from you.

Chapter Fifteen

A Final Thought—Enjoy Yourself

*Human beings are happiest when they
are busy doing something they like.*

Retirement is a unique time. It's a respite, a well-deserved reward for an arduous and sometimes tumultuous journey through life. Those former all-consuming struggles to earn a living, advance one's career, raise a family, and accumulate wealth and assets, many now gathering dust in the garage, basement, or closet, will quickly decrease in importance. Even the burden of taxes becomes lighter as government rebates and pension checks cause money to flow into your pocket instead of out of them.

It also can be a time of self-direction, personal goal-setting, and reassessment of one's values. What is important to you as an individual? What makes you happy? What ideas, things, and activities do you value at this time in your life? And why are you not doing them? At the very least, one of your goals in retirement should be to get out and indulge yourself by doing something that you enjoy.

Although this book presents twelve helpful retirement strategies, five retirement approaches, a balanced lifestyle model, and eighty interesting projects, there is no single blueprint for you to follow. Your journey in this final stage of your life is a very personal, self-directed one, and it comes without instructions. There are no rules on how retirees should behave or what they should be doing. Sixty-five-year-olds can be seen in red sports cars, on escorted tours of China, on country biking trails, at motorcycle conventions, organizing family reunions, refinishing antique furniture, taking T'ai Chi lessons, painting scenic watercolors, and operating their own businesses.

Retirees can look to their friends, neighbors, or parents for models of what to do in retirement, but usually following someone else's dreams and desires never proves to be personally fulfilling, just time filling. The key to happiness is to focus on things that you enjoy doing and to share the love of those activities with your friends.

To achieve some sense of personal fulfillment and enjoyment in retirement, you are going to have to evaluate what you want, explore possibilities, and take risks. People who approach this era with forethought, a bit of discipline, and a sense of adventure can anticipate an enjoyable, memorable, and rewarding retirement.

What retirees lack the most is structure. Most days are undefined with no goals to aim for and no specific tasks to accomplish. Change that situation. Enroll in a hobby course. Join a community group of volunteers or a group of hobby enthusiasts. Plan an inexpensive Elderhostel vacation and combine learning with travel. Being around people will create additional outlets for social interaction. Being with people who enjoy their hobbies will inspire you. Their enthusiasm becomes infectious.

One word of caution. The biggest hindrance to a successful, active, and long retirement will be your health. Build exercise into your daily routine so that your muscles do not atrophy and your bone density doesn't diminish to the point where getting off the couch or walking any distance becomes a major chore. Even moderate, gradual exercise, such as going for walks, swimming, or performing stretching exercises, can maintain muscle and bone density and give you the energy to do other things.

Almost everyone has experienced the postponement of important decisions, or the delay of major changes in one's life, safe in the knowledge that there will always be time in the future to complete those tasks. As retirees, you probably have come to the realization that time is not infinite, that good health, friendships, and opportunities for exploring will diminish with time. Make the best of each day. Human beings are happiest when they are busy doing something they like. Being inactive is depressing and unhealthy.

If you are still unsure of what to do with your retirement, ask yourself this one key question. "What is it that I always wanted to do?" Then, simply, go do it. Have you ever wanted to learn to fly an airplane or learn to speak a foreign language? Have you ever wanted to visit Australia and have your picture taken with some wallabies? If there's anything life has taught you, it's that anything is possible. If other humans have accomplished similar goals, then so can you. Do some research. Find out what it takes financially, physically, and intellectually (reading, courses, workshops) to achieve your goal. Read books about it. Search the Internet for hobbyists who are doing the same thing.

Talk to specialists in the field. Once you are into the research, you are well on your way to reaching your objectives.

One of the paradoxes of retirement is that for the first time in your life, you have the time and the freedom from the demands of a career and from parenting responsibilities to be able to choose any course of action, any hobby, any vacation, any pursuit of happiness that your little heart desires. Simultaneously, it's a time when limitations, such as diminishing health, reduced income, fear of the unknown, and sudden loss of a companion, rise as impediments.

It is imperative, therefore, for retirees to become creative, innovative, and insightful to maximize this once-in-a-lifetime gift of freedom. People in wheelchairs go on ocean cruises. Widows join church travel groups and travel the world. People in their fifties and older often earn university degrees, write books, paint pictures, and photograph exotic wildlife. Countless people who never win the lottery climb aboard their camper trailer and head out to meet people, and experience and photograph the beauty and majesty of the North American continent. Imagine yourself as Don (or Donna) Quixote and his/her sidekick, Sancho Panza, setting off on a grand quest across the countryside in search of adventure, intrigue, romance, and excitement.

Creative retirement involves passion, emotional commitment, and a zest for living. You will encounter those who will resist a high-quality active lifestyle, with remarks like, "You are too old to be doing those things," or "We can't afford it," or "I don't seem to have the energy." Those are excuses of the venerable couch potato. Get off the couch, out of the house, and begin living again. Life is too short and too full of fascinating things to see and do to devote any time to being a vegetable.

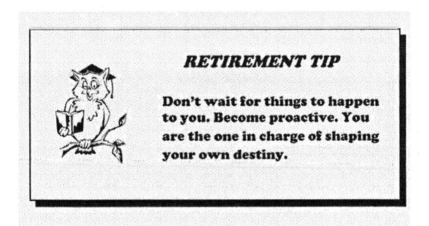

RETIREMENT TIP

Don't wait for things to happen to you. Become proactive. You are the one in charge of shaping your own destiny.

THINGS YOU HAVE ALWAYS WANTED TO DO

In the spaces below, make a list of three things that you have always wanted to do, however improbable those things seemed to you in the earlier stages of your life. Once you have listed them, consider ways to achieve those things with a little planning, and adaptive thinking.

1. _____

2. _____

3. _____

Life Makeovers
By Cheryl Richardson
Broadway Books, 2000
ISBN 0767906632

If you are still having difficulty focusing on what is important to you, you might consider reading this book by a top-level personal coach recommended by Oprah Winfrey. It provides practical, down-to-earth advice along with fifty-two "Take Action" exercises for evaluating, clarifying, and focusing your life. Also available on audio cassette and audio CD for listening to while driving or doing some fitness walking.

TRAVEL REFERENCES FOR RETIREES
Appendix

Unbelievably Good Deals and Great Adventures That You Absolutely Can't Get Unless You're Over 50
by Joan Rattner Heliman
McGraw-Hill, 2001
ISBN   0809294982

Excellent traveler's reference for budget-conscious retirees. Includes adventure travels, special airfares, up to 50 percent off hotels and restaurants. A book from an author who believes things should become cheaper as you become older. Now in its 13th printing.

Travel Unlimited: Uncommon Adventures for the Mature Traveler
by Alison Gardener
Avalon Travel Publishers, 2000
ISBN   1566912121

Travel advice from a veteran globetrotter to kindred spirits who seek a sense of adventure, accomplishment, and fulfillment from their vacations. Details on ecological, educational, cultural, and volunteer vacations ranging from the primitive to luxurious. Inspirational and insightful.

Anyone Can Travel
by Melba Rous, and Eileen Ward
Trafford Publishing, 2000
ISBN 1552123863

A book for seniors with health problems or disabilities written by two registered nurses. Shows the safe and comfortable way to travel. The easy-to-read book is full of practical tips, including planning, booking, traveling by plane, cruise ship, bus, car, and train.

Best Travel Deals
by Consumer Reports
Consumers Union, 2001
ISBN   0890439451

This handy paperback written by the editors of *Consumer Reports Travel Letter* provides travelers with practical advice on the best travel deals on planes, highways, railways, and cruise ships. Also includes tips on using the Internet, coping with seasickness, getting seat and accommodation upgrades. This travel guide is updated each year.

INDEX

A

accreditation committee (genealogy)   190
acrylic painting   114
acting   97
adventure tour   240
altruism   33
antique furniture   300
architectural wonders   90
art   114
aqua fitness   274

B

balanced lifestyle definition   45
ballroom dancing   258
Battle of Gettysburg   184
bird watching   244
Board of Certification (genealogy)   192
bowling   142
bridge player   195

C

camping   225
campground directory   226
campus community   171
card party   140
caregiver services   293

certified genealogist   190
changing your lifestyle   48
chat rooms   146
choral group   159
church auxiliary   144, 208
college degree   171
create your own video/DVD   111
cruise lines, recommended   151
cruising   149

D

dancing   160, 258
deferred retirement   29
delivery for pharmacy   298
designing your own website   124
different expectations (spouses)   38
Doctors Without Borders   200

E

Elderhostel   166
extended vacations   85
exercise equipment   271

F

family history book   108
Familyhostel   168
family reunion   67
fitness club   264
food banks   218
forced into retirement   39
furniture restoration   117

G

gardening	251
garage sale	79
genealogy	108
Global Volunteers	200
golfing	235
grandkids on vacation	152
group trip	76

H

Habitat For Humanity	201
handicraft hobbies	127
hobby course instructor	73
hospital, hospice	203
houseboat	254
house swap	94
housesitter	295
humaine society	216

I

indoor walking	269
Interhostel	167
Internet as a research tool	177

K

Kampgrounds of America, Inc. (KOA)	225

L

leaving a legacy	32
leisure and recreation	30

line dancing   260

M

Meals on Wheels   218
motorcycle rally   223
motorhome   232
Mount Rushmore   92
musical group   304
musical instrument   104

N

National Institute for Genealogy Studies   193
natural light photography   121
nature photography   121
nature walks   276
natural wonders of the world   90
needlecraft artwork   127
need for people   46
new career   286
nonfiction writing   174
nourishing the body, mind, soul   44-46

O

Old Faithful   93
oil painting   114

P

painting	114
photography	120, 159, 247

R

reading as a hobby	181
redecorate and refurbish	100
refinishing antique furniture	300
relationships	36
researching family trees	298
research using Internet	177
retirement communities	132
remodeling retirement home	81
retiring single from a career	40
Routes to Learning Canada	166
run for charity	220

S

search engines	178
seven wonders of the world	90
senior centers	156, 214
seniors websites	148
shut-ins	210
shuttle driver	291
singles websites	138
social activity committee	71
soul mate1	36
square dancing	258
stained glass making	127
strength training	271
Star Trek conventions	158

supper club   88

T

T'ai Chi   261
teach tennis, golf   302
tennis as a sport   282
theater for seniors   97
trip with a theme   76
travel escort   289
traveling alone, resources for   230
TraveLearn   170
travel photography   121
twelve retirement strategies   20

U

unfinished business   31
unusual vacations   77
unwanted shadow   37

V

videography   111
visiting shut-ins   210
virtual universities   172
volunteer career skills   199

W

Walt Disney Cruise Lines   153
walking program   267, 276
watercolor painting   115
Washington, D.C.   181
website design   124

women traveling alone   228
wonders of the world   90
Woodall Campground Directory   226
woodworking   128
wrap gifts for charity   212
writing a family history book   108, 174
writing non-fiction   174

Y

Y.M.C.A.   274

About the Author

Rob Kelley
B.A. M.Ed.

Former teacher, department head, computer education consultant, and textbook author, Rob retired at age fifty to set off in a new direction. "Unfortunately, I turned into a couch potato that first year. When you retire, your daily routine, mental and physical activities, and camaraderie at work all suddenly disappear. Searching for activities that were personally fulfilling and not just time-filling became my goal. I feverently believe that any retiree with a little reflection on what they enjoy the most, and some creative thinking on how to obtain their goals, can enjoy an immensely rewarding retirement. I also believe that age, wealth, and education are only limiting factors if you chose to perceive them as roadblocks, Those who remain young at heart will enjoy new adventures well into their eighties.

True to his beliefs, Rob has since researched and written two family history books, joined the gym, been on two ocean cruises, attended photography workshops in Florida and South Carolina, annual writing workshops in California, organized a family tree reunion, and taught himself how to play the piano. His most passionate hobby, however, is writing books. He lives in a steel-manufacturing, university town, home of the Hamilton Tiger Cats and Copps Coliseum, in Hamilton, Ontario, Canada.

Printed in the United States
33855LVS00003B/319-330